SIMON & SCHUSTER BOOKS FOR YOUNG READERS
An imprint of Simon & Schuster Children's Publishing Division
1230 Avenue of the Americas, New York, New York 10020

Conceived and produced by Weldon Owen Pty Ltd
59–61 Victoria Street, McMahons Point
Sydney NSW 2060, Australia

Copyright © 2008 Weldon Owen Pty Ltd
Originally published in Great Britain in 2008
by the Templar Company Limited
First U.S. edition 2009

WELDON OWEN GROUP
Chairman John Owen

WELDON OWEN PTY LTD
Chief Executive Officer Sheena Coupe
Creative Director Sue Burk
Publisher Margaret Whiskin
Senior Vice President, International Sales Stuart Laurence
Vice President, Sales: United States and Canada Amy Kaneko
Vice President, Sales: Asia and Latin America Dawn Low
Administration Manager, International Sales Kristine Ravn
Production Manager Todd Rechner
Production Coordinators Lisa Conway, Mike Crowton

Editor Lachlan McLaine
Designer Kathryn Morgan
Cover Design Kathryn Morgan, Sarah Norton, Juliana Titin
Art Manager Trucie Henderson
Content Provider Charles O. Hyman
DVD Production A La Carte Communications
Editorial Coordinator Hunnah Jessup

Color reproduction by Chroma Graphics (Overseas) Pte Ltd
Printed by SNP Leefung Printers Ltd
Manufactured in China

A WELDON OWEN PRODUCTION

SIMON & SCHUSTER BOOKS FOR YOUNG READERS
is a trademark of Simon & Schuster, Inc.
The text for this book is set in Glypha and Univers.
10 9 8 7 6 5 4 3 2 1
Cataloging-in-publication data for this book is available
from the Library of Congress.

ISBN: 978-1-4169-7935-7

Simon & Schuster Books for Young Readers
New York London Toronto Sydney

MISSION TO THE
MOON

Alan Dyer

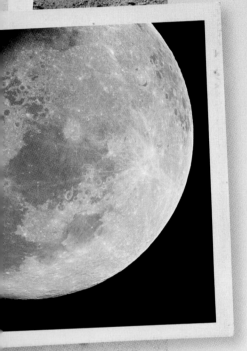

Contents

MISSION: MOON

The Moon and Us.............8

Moon Myths 10

Reaching for the Moon...12

The Space Race Begins..14

America Responds.........16

Machines to the Moon....18

Aiming for the Moon 20

The Cape 22

Selecting and Training
    Astronauts.................24

Practice in the Field.......26

Apollo Chronology.........28

Saturn V Rocket 30

Countdown....................32

Liftoff! 34

Mission Control.............36

Journey to the Moon 38

Touchdown 40

Lunar Module.................42

Exploring the Surface:
    Apollo 11 44

Exploring the Surface:
    Later Missions 46

On the Moon 48

Space Suit.....................50

Lunar Rover...................52

Command Module Pilot..54

Splashdown 56

Apollo 13.......................58

Moon Rock....................60

After Apollo...................62

Back to the Moon? 64

Moon Base....................66

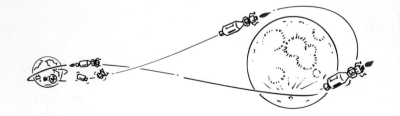

ALL ABOUT THE MOON

The Earth–Moon System..70

Phases of the Moon 72

Moon Structure 74

Surface Features 76

Glossary..........................78

Index 80

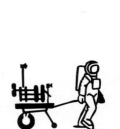

Mission: Moon

The Moon and Us

The Moon has always inspired us to look skyward. Since prehistoric times, every culture around the world has looked to the Moon, used it to tell time, and wondered how it came to be in our sky. What was this object that changed shape, disappeared, then returned each month to rule the night? Was this a home for the gods? Or could people one day reach for the Moon and actually go there? This is the story of how our dream of Moon travel came true in our own time. It is the story of epic voyages planned and completed by people alive today. It is the story of the Apollo missions to the Moon.

Stone Age Moon
This row of dots was painted on the wall of Lascaux Cave in France 17,000 years ago. Some researchers think that the dots are a record of the monthly cycle of the Moon.

The Nebra sky disk
About 3,600 years ago people in Europe may have used this bronze disk featuring a gold Moon, Sun, and stars to help them create an accurate annual calendar.

Moon Myths

For thousands of years the Moon has been seen as a place of myth and legend, of good and evil. The Sumerians who lived 4,500 years ago thought that the souls of the dead went to the Moon and descended to the underworld for judgment during the New Moon phase—when the Moon's face was completely in shadow and seemed to disappear into the darkness. Later cultures, such as the ancient Greeks and Romans, worshipped the Moon as the goddess of birth and fertility, and the protector of animals. Medieval superstitions claimed that the Moon's light caused "lunacy," or madness. Even today, people often blame "loony" behavior on the Full Moon, but scientific studies have shown that there is no link.

Beyond the sky
This woodcut from the 1800s shows the earlier Medieval belief that the sky was the surface of a "celestial sphere" that lay like an upturned bowl on a flat Earth. Cosmic machinery behind the sphere was thought to keep the Moon, Sun, and stars in motion.

NAMES OF THE MOON
The original Greek Moon goddess was Selene. In Roman mythology she was called Luna (from which we get our words "lunar" and "lunacy"), then was later known as Diana. However, NASA's Apollo Moon program was named after the Greek god of light, truth, and the Sun. Apollo was the twin brother of Artemis, another ancient Moon goddess.

Selene in Greece
The goddess Selene fell in love with the mortal Endymion, the first human to observe the cycles of the Moon. The gods placed him into an eternal sleep.

Baboon Moon
Thoth, the ancient Egyptian Moon god, was sometimes depicted as a wise baboon because baboons "sang" to the Moon at night.

Aztec Moon
In Aztec tradition from ancient Mexico, the gods hurled a rabbit toward the newly created Moon and its unmarked face, creating the shapes we see today.

IMAGINING THE MOON

People have long looked at the Moon and seen mythological creatures drawn by the Moon's dark "seas." We now know that these seas are smooth lava plains.

Man in the Moon
People in Europe and North America see the face of a man in the Moon.

Moon man down under
From the southern hemisphere the Moon appears inverted, so a different face is seen.

Rabbit and egg
Anglo-Saxon myths tell of a rabbit carrying an egg, both symbols for life, birth, and spring.

Witch in the Moon
In the 1500s people in England saw a witch or an old man carrying a bundle of sticks.

Toad in the Moon
Chinese legends tell of a woman, Chang'e, who fled to the Moon and was turned into a toad.

Crab in the Moon
People living on islands in the South Pacific see an ocean crab in the Moon's markings.

Moonwitches
Witches were believed to draw upon the power of the Moon goddess for conducting their wicked rituals.

Lunar werewolves
According to legend, werewolves change from human to howling wolf under the evil light of the Full Moon.

Reaching for the Moon

Since the dawn of civilization people around the world have used the monthly cycle of the Moon's phases to help count time and create a calendar. But they had little idea what the Moon actually was. A god? A glowing cosmic sphere? An unreachable part of heaven? It was not until the 1600s, when the Moon was first observed with telescopes, that people realized it was a world like Earth, with rugged mountains and volcanic plains, and close enough that we might reach it one day. That dream became the ultimate goal of inventors in the early 1900s, who knew that the only way to reach the Moon was to propel through space with rockets.

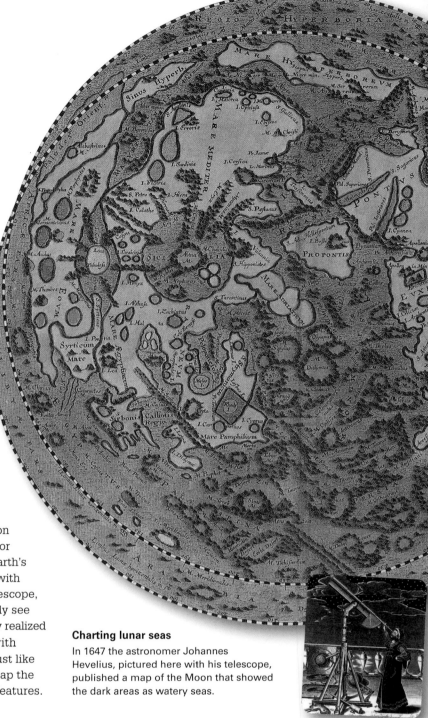

Ptolemy's cosmos
Ancient Greek astronomer Ptolemy concluded that all worlds revolved around Earth. In his time the heavens, Moon, and planets were thought to be made of a substance called "quintessence."

EXPLORING A NEW WORLD

For hundreds of years people thought the Moon might be a smooth mirror reflecting an image of Earth's continents. From 1609, with the invention of the telescope, astronomers could finally see the Moon close-up. They realized it was another world with mountains and plains just like Earth. They began to map the Moon and name these features.

Charting lunar seas
In 1647 the astronomer Johannes Hevelius, pictured here with his telescope, published a map of the Moon that showed the dark areas as watery seas.

Copernicus
In 1543 the Polish astronomer Nicholas Copernicus challenged centuries of thinking. He proposed that Earth and the other planets revolved around the Sun, and only the Moon orbited Earth.

First Moon maps
In 1609 Italian Galileo Galilei became the first person to study the Moon through a telescope. He sketched these images to record the mountains and craters that he saw.

AIM FOR THE MOON

By the late 1800s writers began to imagine ways we could travel to the Moon, though by then people realized the Moon was airless and lifeless.

Moon mission, 1865

French writer Jules Verne, in his novel *From the Earth to the Moon*, imagined three astronauts propelled to the Moon in a capsule launched from Florida. This was a remarkable prediction that came true a century later.

Moon mission, 1930

This comic strip shows astronauts flying to the Moon then sending signals back to Earth with a powerful searchlight.

War rockets

Captured by Allied troops at the end of World War II, Nazi V-2 rocket missiles were the first rockets used in the American and Soviet space programs.

ROCKET SCIENCE

By the 1900s people knew that fuel would not burn in airless space, so the only way to travel to the Moon was to use a rocket that carried its own oxygen supply.

Rocket pioneers

In the early 1900s Konstantin Tsiolkovskii in Russia, left, and Robert Goddard in the United States, above, designed the first liquid-fueled rockets, but only Goddard flew them.

The Space Race Begins

In the 1950s and 1960s, the Soviet Union (what is now Russia and its surrounding countries) and the United States were locked in a cold war. They fought each other not with weapons and soldiers but with threats and demonstrations of power. Both countries were building rockets that could deliver nuclear bombs. On October 4, 1957, the Soviet Union used one of these rockets to launch a probe called Sputnik 1 into orbit around Earth. This was the first artificial satellite. The achievement shocked the world and started the space race. The Soviets took the lead with the first animal in space (in November, 1957), the first man in space (in 1961), the first woman in space (in 1963), and the first space walk (in 1965).

COLD WAR PROPAGANDA

Both U.S. and Soviet politicians used their space programs as propaganda. Any achievements in space were held up as proof that their political system and technology were superior.

YURI GAGARIN

To be the first to enter the cosmos, to engage, single-handed, in an unprecedented duel with nature— could one dream of anything more?

BEFORE HIS FLIGHT INTO SPACE, 1961

Yuri Gagarin: first human in space
Imagine being the first to ride an explosive rocket into space, where some said no one could survive. On April 12, 1961, Soviet cosmonaut Yuri Gagarin braved the dangers to become the first person in space. His flight around the world lasted 108 minutes.

ANIMALS IN ORBIT

Before risking people, both the United States and the Soviet Union sent animals into space. Monkeys, chimpanzees, and small dogs all made the journey. Some did not survive because of equipment malfunctions, but most returned safely to Earth, proving humans could do so as well.

THE U.S. FLOPNIK

Two months after Sputnik 1 flew into space, the United States attempted to launch its first satellite, Vanguard. Millions watched on television as the rocket exploded on the launch pad. It was a very public and humiliating failure for the new U.S. space program.

Out of the ashes
The Vanguard program included eleven attempted satellite launches. Only three were successful. These three satellites are still orbiting Earth today.

The first spacecraft
Yuri Gagarin and other early Soviet cosmonauts flew in a one-person spacecraft called Vostok (Russian for "east"), riding in a spherical capsule.

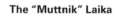

Sputnik 1
The first artificial satellite was a small metallic ball with four whisker-like antennae and a radio transmitter.

The "Muttnik" Laika
In November 1957 Sputnik 2 carried the dog Laika, the first animal in orbit. Sadly, the Soviets had no way to bring her back—she died in space.

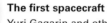

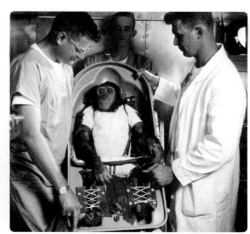

Ham the Astrochimp
In January 1961 Ham became the first hominid to fly into space. He safely came back from his 17-minute flight, and lived, well cared for, until 1983.

America Responds

In 1961 the Cold War was at its height. America could not let the Soviet Union and its communist government take the lead in space. In May, U.S. president John F. Kennedy proclaimed: "I believe that this nation should commit itself to achieving the goal, before this decade is out, of landing a man on the Moon and returning him safely to the Earth." Considering America's only manned mission to date was Alan Shepard's 15-minute Mercury flight three weeks earlier, landing men on the Moon in just seven years was an ambitious goal. But the fear was, if America did not do it, the Soviet Union, then well ahead in the space race, certainly would.

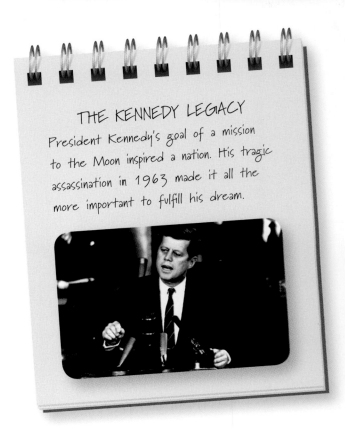

THE KENNEDY LEGACY
President Kennedy's goal of a mission to the Moon inspired a nation. His tragic assassination in 1963 made it all the more important to fulfill his dream.

THE MERCURY SEVEN

America selected its first astronauts from hundreds of military test pilots. On April 9, 1959, seven astronauts with the "right stuff" were announced (from left to right): Walter Schirra, Alan Shepard, Deke Slayton, Gus Grissom, John Glenn, Gordon Cooper, and Scott Carpenter. Of the "Original 7," Schirra, Shepard, and Slayton also flew on Apollo but only Shepard went to the Moon.

Mercury training
The Mercury astronauts trained intensively for their missions. Training took place in the air, in simulators, and in the wilderness (in case they landed in a jungle or desert).

First American in orbit
On February 20, 1962, John Glenn became the first American to orbit Earth in a five-hour mission in his Mercury capsule, Friendship 7. He also flew on the Space Shuttle in 1998, becoming, at age 77, the oldest astronaut ever to fly.

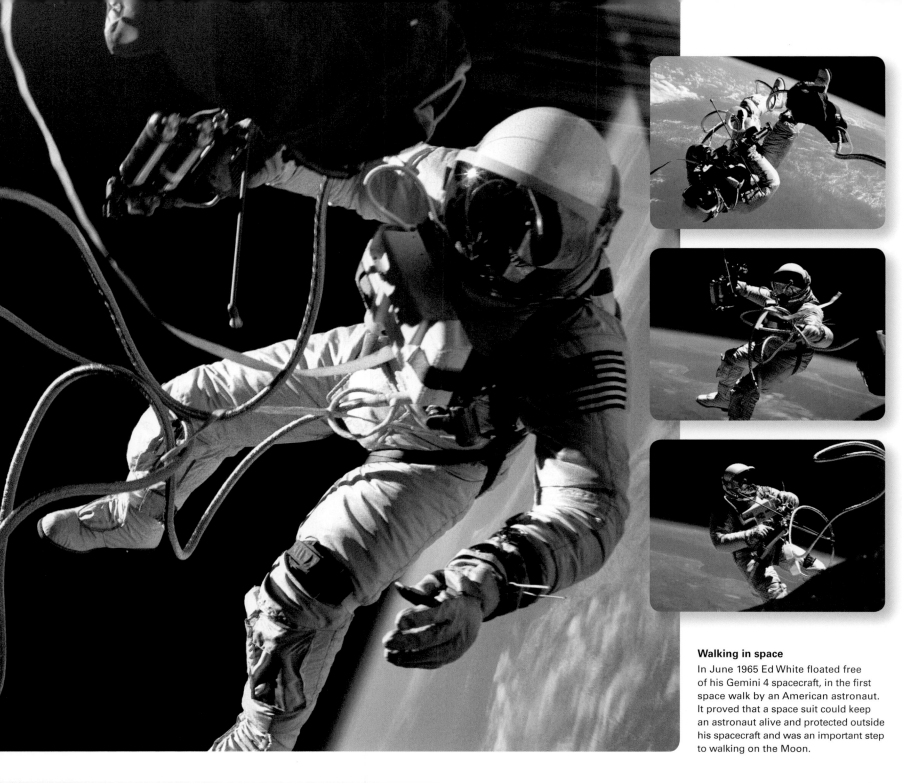

Walking in space

In June 1965 Ed White floated free of his Gemini 4 spacecraft, in the first space walk by an American astronaut. It proved that a space suit could keep an astronaut alive and protected outside his spacecraft and was an important step to walking on the Moon.

GEMINI

After the one-man Mercury missions, NASA launched a series of Gemini spacecraft in 1965 and 1966, each with two astronauts aboard. The ten Gemini missions perfected rendezvous and docking methods needed for a Moon mission and tested astronauts' ability to live and work in space.

Docking practice

Using a mechanical simulator on Earth, Gemini astronauts practiced their techniques for flying and docking their spacecraft.

Titan liftoff

Every two or three months a Gemini Titan rocket launched from Cape Canaveral carrying two astronauts into Earth orbit.

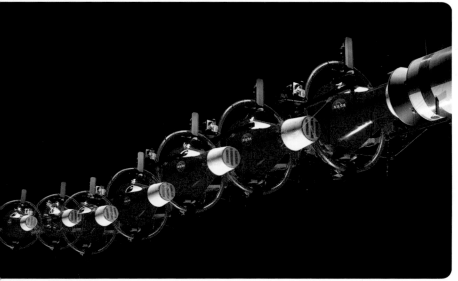

Machines to the Moon

Before Apollo, scientists knew so little about the Moon that some feared a spacecraft visiting the Moon might sink into deep lunar dust. To learn if people could land safely, the Soviet Union and United States first sent unmanned robot probes as part of their race to the Moon. The Soviets had the first successes: in September 1959 their Luna 2 probe became the first human-made object to hit the Moon; in October 1959 Luna 3 returned the first photos of the Moon's far side; and in February 1966 Luna 9 performed the first soft landing. But NASA soon caught up, launching their Ranger, Surveyor, and Lunar Orbiter probes.

Moon stamps
In October 1959 Luna 3 flew around the far side of the Moon and returned the first images of the unseen side of the Moon, a mission commemorated in these Soviet stamps.

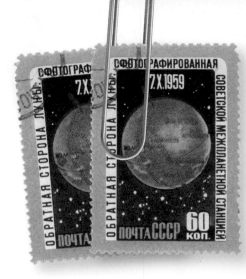

ORBITER

From 1966 to 1967 NASA's five Lunar Orbiter probes circled the Moon, together mapping and photographing 99 percent of the surface. The images helped scientists select landing sites for the manned Apollo missions that followed two years later.

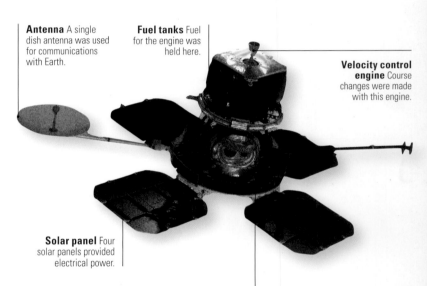

Antenna A single dish antenna was used for communications with Earth.

Fuel tanks Fuel for the engine was held here.

Velocity control engine Course changes were made with this engine.

Solar panel Four solar panels provided electrical power.

Photographic system The Orbiters processed photographic film on board, scanned it, and transmitted the images back to Earth.

RANGER

In 1964 and 1965 the American Ranger 7, 8, and 9 probes were deliberately crashed into the Moon. In the minutes and final seconds before impact they returned hundreds of ever-closer images of the surface. These showed craters of every size, down to as small as a few feet across.

Moonstruck
In the 1960s moonstruck kids stayed up late to watch television pictures beamed back from the Ranger probes, the first live television broadcasts from the Moon. They saw the Moon getting closer and closer, until—impact!

Camera aperture
The Ranger probes housed six separate camera systems.

Solar panels These provided electric power to the spacecraft.

Photo of the century
When this spectacular image of the crater Copernicus was beamed back by Lunar Orbiter 2 in November 1966 it was called the "photo of the century"—no one had ever seen the Moon in such detail before.

LUNA

The Luna program was a Soviet series of robotic spacecraft launched at the Moon between 1959 and 1976. Fifteen succeeded in either flying by the Moon, entering its orbit, crashing into it, or making a soft landing. To perform its pioneering soft landing, Luna 9 capsule was contained inside an inflated air bag that popped off the main craft just above the surface.

Luna 9 landing

1 The Luna 9 spacecraft approaches the Moon's surface. A main retrorocket slows the descent. Smaller rocket engines keep it upright.
2 A contact rod touches the surface, triggering the release of the air bag.
3 When it has come to rest the air bag explodes apart, revealing the egg-shaped capsule inside.
4 The capsule is weighted to right itself. Once it does, its petals spring open and it begins to transmit images of the surface back to Earth.

SURVEYOR

From 1966 to 1968 NASA launched seven unmanned Surveyor probes, each designed to soft land on the Moon and send back panoramic images of its landing site. Some probes also had a robotic arm to scoop into the soil to determine how soft the surface was.

Visiting an old friend

In November 1969 astronauts Pete Conrad and Alan Bean of Apollo 12 set down near the Surveyor 3 probe, which had landed in April 1967, to see what 30 months of exposure to space had done to the robot spacecraft.

Aiming for the Moon

In the early 1960s engineers had only just learned how to launch someone into space. No one knew how to get astronauts all the way to the Moon—and back! At first, people thought one huge spaceship would be best. It would do it all: fly to the Moon, land, take off, and return. However, that method needed a rocket and a spacecraft so large and complex neither could have been built in time to meet President Kennedy's goal of landing on the Moon by 1969. In the end, the chosen two-spacecraft method worked so well that future lunar missions now being planned will use a similar method for landing on the Moon.

MOON MISSION CHOICES

NASA considered three methods of getting astronauts to the Moon and back. The first two were too costly, requiring too large a rocket or lander. The third method was more risky but achievable by the end of the 1960s.

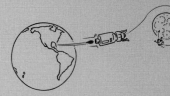
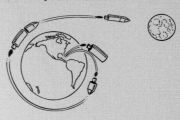

Direct ascent
One giant five-stage rocket launches. The top two stages land; one stage returns.

Earth orbit rendezvous
The spacecraft and a fuel tank launch separately. The single large craft lands and returns.

Lunar orbit rendezvous
The chosen method used a lightweight lander and spacecraft in lunar orbit.

LEAVING EARTH

GETTING TO THE MOON

The system NASA chose for the lunar landings employed two specialized spacecraft: one that orbited the Moon and returned to Earth (the Command/Service Module), and a second small one that landed on and lifted off the Moon (the Lunar Module). Each carried exactly the amount of rocket fuel needed for its job, keeping the size and cost of each craft as low as possible.

Liftoff
The three-stage Saturn V rocket, with the Command, Service, and Lunar modules on top, takes off from Cape Canaveral, placing the craft and crew into orbit around Earth.

Translunar injection
The first and second stages of the Saturn V fall back to Earth. After one orbit of Earth, the third-stage engine fires to propel the spacecraft toward the Moon.

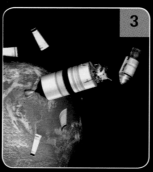

Transposition and docking
The crew detach the combined Command/Service Module, turn it around, then pull the Lunar Module from the third stage. The discarded third stage goes on to hit the Moon.

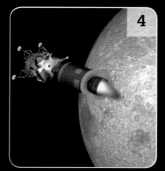

Lunar orbit insertion
Three days later the Service Module's main engine slows down the Apollo craft so it enters orbit around the Moon instead of flying off into space or returning to Earth.

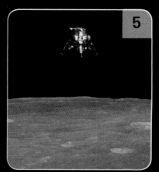

Descent to the Moon
The Lunar Module, with two astronauts aboard, separates and lands on the Moon, leaving the third crew member in orbit in the Command/Service Module.

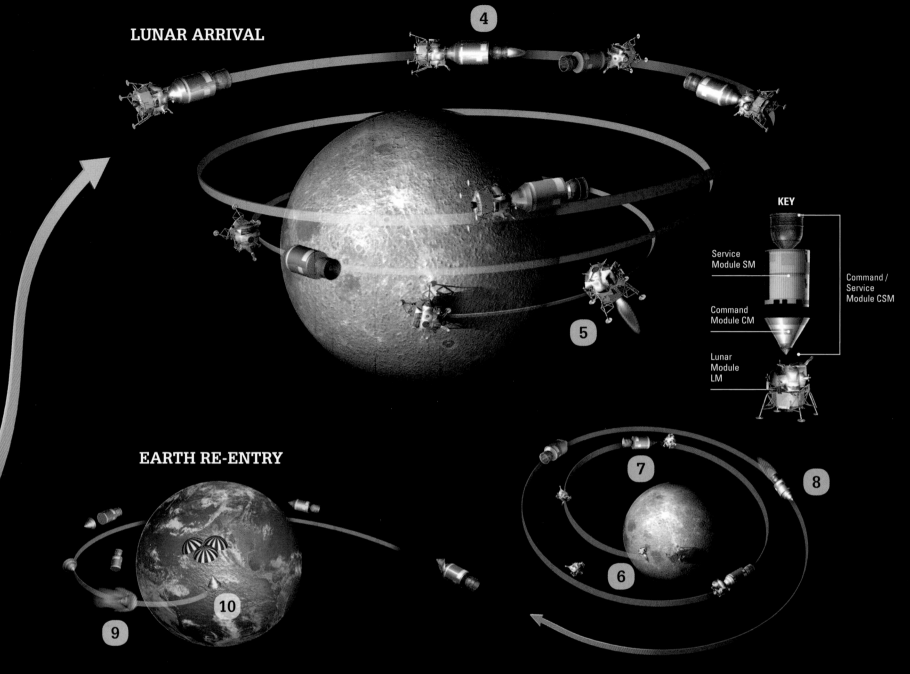

LUNAR ARRIVAL

KEY

Service
Module SM

Command /
Service
Module CSM

Command
Module CM

Lunar
Module
LM

EARTH RE-ENTRY

LEAVING THE MOON

Ascent stage liftoff
After exploring the Moon, the astronauts return to the top half of the Lunar Module. This Ascent Stage has its own rocket and blasts off the Moon. The bottom half is left behind.

Redocking in lunar orbit
The Ascent Stage of the Lunar Module re-docks with the Command Module where the astronauts are reunited. The Ascent Stage is discarded and hits the Moon.

Transearth injection
With all three astronauts aboard the spacecraft, the Service Module's main engine fires again to power the craft away from the Moon and back toward Earth for the three-day journey home.

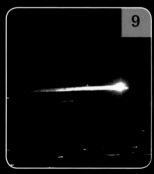

Re-entry
When reaching Earth, the Command Module separates from the Service Module. Both re-enter, but only the Command Module, with its heat shield for protection, survives.

Splashdown
The Command Module falls through the atmosphere and parachutes open to slow its descent. The craft splashes down, usually in the Pacific, where an aircraft carrier picks up the crew.

The Cape

After World War II the U.S. government looked for a site to test its missiles, including the captured German V-2 rockets. It chose a sandy spit of land on the east coast of Florida called Cape Canaveral and in 1950 construction began on what later became known as the Kennedy Space Center. Rockets take off to the east of the Cape, over the ocean, in case a rocket explodes and falls to Earth. At a latitude of 28.5 degrees north, Cape Canaveral is closer to the equator than most other places in the United States. Because Earth's rotation speed increases toward the equator, this launch site offers extra velocity to a rocket, helping it to reach orbit using less fuel and carrying more payload.

JULY 24, 1950
Bumper V-2 liftoff. The first missile launch at Cape Canaveral.

Cape from space
A view from orbit shows Cape Canaveral, with its many pads, runways, service buildings, and a seaport. It is separated from the Florida mainland by a lagoon.

The biggest building
Assembling the Saturn V rockets required one of the world's largest enclosed spaces, the Vehicle Assembly Building. It was constructed in the mid-1960s and the first rocket rolled out in May 1966.

Launch control 1950s style
While Apollo launches required hundreds of technicians, the first rocket launches from Cape Canaveral were watched over by just a handful of scientists in small concrete blockhouses near the launch pad.

WILDLIFE AND ROCKETS

The large undeveloped safety zone around Cape Canaveral became a national wildlife refuge. Some 500 species of birds, mammals, and reptiles live in the refuge's 140,000 acres (57,000 ha) of salty marshes, sand dunes, and pine forests.

Alligator
Nearly 5,000 freshwater alligators live in the Cape's ponds and waterways.

Missile row
In addition to pads for large manned rockets (and now the Space Shuttle), Cape Canaveral has many pads for the smaller rockets used to launch space probes and satellites, including military craft.

Eagles and dolphins
Bald eagles nest in the Cape's forests and migrating dolphins swim in its coastal waters.

Selecting and Training Astronauts

Because no one knew what ordeals astronauts would have to endure during the first space missions, NASA chose its first astronauts from the ranks of test pilots. These were men with the "right stuff" who bravely tested new or experimental aircraft by pushing them to extremes. They were used to flying complex machines and handling sudden crises when aircraft went out of control. Only later, in the mid-1960s, were a few scientists chosen to be astronauts. Of all the Apollo astronauts, only Harrison Schmitt was a trained geologist and he flew on Apollo 17, the last Moon mission. He helped train other moonwalkers in geology but he also had to learn to fly a jet so he could serve as Lunar Module pilot.

ROCKET PLANE PILOT
Before he ventured into space, Neil Armstrong flew the experimental X-15 rocket aircraft.

SIMULATING SPACE

Astronauts on the Moon felt only one-sixth the weight they did on Earth. On the way to the Moon they experienced weightlessness, known as "zero-g," or zero gravity. At other times—under the stress of "high-g" launches and landings—astronauts felt many times their own weight. Clever methods were devised to simulate what they would feel under zero-, high-, and low-g conditions.

Zero-g aircraft
Aircraft flying up and down in roller-coaster-like flight paths provided brief moments of low- or zero-g, long enough to test equipment.

Spinning centrifuge
Spinning astronauts at high speed pushed them back into their seats to simulate the high-g forces of launch or landing.

Wall walker
Astronaut trainees were suspended sideways on wires to simulate the experience of walking along a surface in reduced gravity.

LEFT ON EARTH

In the early 1960s thirteen women passed all the physical tests required to become an astronaut, often enduring the punishing trials better than did male candidates. But the tests were not official and NASA was not ready for women astronauts. It ruled that only test pilots could become astronauts. American women did not fly into space until the 1980s.

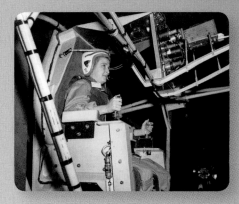

Tumble training
Jerrie Cobb, one of the women put through the Mercury astronaut tests, "flies" a spinning gyro chair that simulates a tumbling spacecraft.

Thrill ride
Astronauts called it the "flying bedstead." They used this rocket-powered Lunar Landing Research Vehicle (LLRV) to practice flying the Lunar Module. Several crashed and, on one practice run, Neil Armstrong narrowly avoided death when he ejected from an out-of-control LLRV at the last moment.

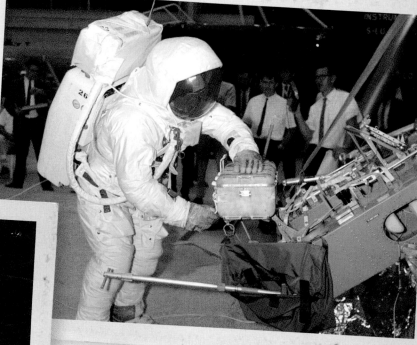

MOONWALK REHEARSALS

Every movement, every task, and every piece of equipment used during moonwalks had to be tested and practiced over and over again on Earth. A moonwalk lasted just a few hours on the Moon but it required hundreds of hours of training and cost hundreds of millions of dollars. No one wanted mistakes!

Practice in the Field

Training for the Apollo missions did not only take place in simulators and indoor test labs. Astronauts also practiced their moonwalking and rock-hunting skills in barren deserts, craters, and volcanic lava fields on Earth. Geologists taught them all about types of rocks and explained how the landscape around them might have formed. Other fieldwork included survival training, in case they landed in the wrong place back on Earth and had to survive for days before being rescued. That never happened, but astronauts had to train for every possible emergency that mission planners could think of.

Moonscape on Earth
In the barren landscape of Cinder Lake, near Flagstaff, Arizona, NASA blasted out small craters with explosives to simulate a moonscape. Here, astronauts practiced with the suits, tools, and Rovers they would use on the Moon. The site is still used to test robotic rovers and equipment bound for Mars.

Driver training
In 1970, a year before their Apollo 15 mission, David Scott and Jim Irwin test-drove a mock-up Rover around the artificial craters at the Cinder Lake test site in Arizona. They were the first crew to use a Lunar Rover.

ROCK SCHOOL

Geologists took astronauts to places such as the Grand Canyon and Meteor Crater in Arizona and to moonlike landscapes in Canada and Iceland. Astronauts learned how to quickly identify the rocks that would provide the best evidence for how the Moon formed.

SPACE MISSION SURVIVAL

Astronauts did survival training in deserts and jungles in case they landed off course when they returned to Earth. In the deserts of the western United States, they learned how to turn their parachutes into clothing to protect them from the Sun. In the jungles of Panama, they made shelters and lived off the land.

Apollo Chronology

The Apollo Moon program began in the early 1960s. From 1969 through 1972, nine missions—Apollo 8, Apollo 10, and Apollo 11 through 17—flew to the Moon. There were plans for three more missions—Apollo 18, 19, and 20—and Saturn V rockets were built for them. These missions might have gone to sites such as the huge craters Copernicus and Tycho, perhaps with astronauts using lunar flying vehicles. However, one Saturn V was needed to launch Skylab, the first space station in 1973. The other two planned missions were canceled because of cuts to NASA budgets. Apollo spacecraft flew Earth orbit missions from 1973 through 1975, taking astronauts to visit Skylab and to dock with a Soviet Soyuz spacecraft.

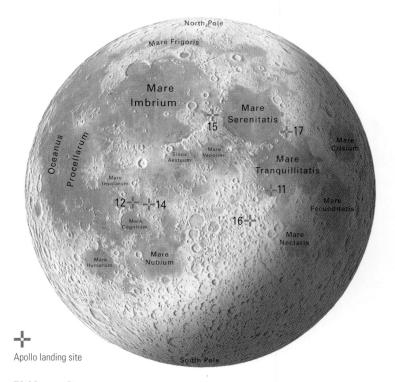

✛
Apollo landing site

Picking a site
Landing sites needed a safe approach path for the Lunar Module and level ground for landing. All sites were close to the equator to minimize the amount of fuel needed to enter and leave lunar orbit. Sites were also chosen because of their geology. Scientists wanted samples from a variety of formations such as younger volcanic plains and ancient highlands.

KEY	
C Commander	**LMP** Lunar Module pilot
CMP Command Module pilot	
△ Command Module call sign	🌑 Lunar Module call sign
🚀 Launch	🌑 Lunar Landing	⛱ Splashdown
🛺 Distance traveled on Moon	∞ Mass of samples collected
Mission summary and key facts	

MISSION INSIGNIA

APOLLO 7	
C Walter Shirra	**LMP** Walter Cunningham
CMP Don Eisele	
△ none	🌑 n/a
🚀 Oct. 11, 1968	⛱ Oct. 22, 1968

Earth orbit mission. The first manned mission of the Apollo program. First U.S. three-man space mission.

APOLLO 1	
C Virgil "Gus" Grissom	**Senior pilot** Edward White
Pilot Roger Chafee	
△ none	🌑 n/a
🚀 Feb. 21, 1967 (planned)	⛱ March 7, 1967 (planned)

Scheduled as first manned Apollo mission. All crew killed in a fire during a ground test.

APOLLO 8	
C Frank Borman	**LMP** William Anders
CMP James Lovell, Jnr.	
△ none	🌑 n/a
🚀 Dec. 21, 1968	⛱ Dec. 27, 1968

First manned mission to leave Earth orbit. First humans to go around the Moon. First manned launch by Saturn V rocket.

FACT FILE

The first manned Apollo mission was Apollo 7. Before that came Apollo 1, in 1967. This would have been the first manned flight in the program. It turned to tragedy when the crew, Gus Grissom, Ed White, and Roger Chaffee, were killed in a fire in the Command Module during a test on the launch pad. Apollo 2 through 6 were test launches of the rockets and spacecraft without any crew aboard.

No man mission
This is the mission insignia for Apollo 5, an unmanned test flight of the Lunar Module in January 1968.

1967 Three astronauts die in the Apollo 1 tragedy.

1961 President Kennedy pledges to put a man on the Moon "by the end of this decade."

1968 Apollo 8—first manned flight to the Moon and back.

APOLLO 9

C James McDivitt   **LMP** Russell "Rusty" Schweikart
CMP David Scott

△ Gumdrop   🕷 Spider

🚀 Mar. 3, 1969   ⏳ Mar. 13, 1969

Earth orbit mission. First flight test of the Lunar Module and first test of the Portable Life Support System in space.

APOLLO 10

C Thomas Stafford   **LMP** Eugene Cernan
CMP John Young

△ Charlie Brown   🕷 Snoopy

🚀 May 18, 1969   ⏳ May 26, 1969

Dress rehearsal for the first manned lunar landing. Lunar Module descended to within 8.5 miles (14 km) of the Moon's surface.

APOLLO 11

C Neil Armstrong   **LMP** Edwin "Buzz" Aldrin
CMP Michael Collins

△ Columbia   🕷 Eagle

🚀 Jul. 16, 1969   🧑‍🚀 Jul. 20, 1969   ⏳ Jul. 24, 1969

🚶 ~270 yards (250 m)   ◯◯ 47.8 pounds (21.7 kg)

First space mission to land people on another world. First return of samples from another planetary body.

APOLLO 12

C Charles Conrad, Jr.   **LMP** Alan Bean
CMP Richard Gordon

△ Yankee Clipper   🕷 Intrepid

🚀 Nov. 14, 1969   🧑‍🚀 Nov. 19, 1969   ⏳ Nov. 24, 1969

🚶 0.9 mile (1.5 km)   ◯◯ 75.6 pounds (34.3 kg)

Mission almost aborted after the Command Module was twice struck by lightning during the first minute after liftoff.

APOLLO 13

C James Lovell, Jr.   **LMP** Fred Haise
CMP John "Jack" Swigert

△ Odyssey   🕷 Aquarius

🚀 Apr. 11, 1970   🧑‍🚀 did not land   ⏳ Apr. 17, 1970

Moon landing canceled after an explosion in the Service Module. The crew were lucky to make it back alive.

APOLLO 14

C Alan Shepard   **LMP** Edgar Mitchell
CMP Stuart Roosa

△ Kitty Hawk   🕷 Antares

🚀 Jan. 31, 1971   🧑‍🚀 Feb. 5, 1971   ⏳ Feb. 9, 1971

🚶 2 miles (3.3 km)   ◯◯ 98.8 pounds (44.8 kg)

Landed at the site intended for the Apollo 13 mission. First experiments conducted by Command Module pilot in lunar orbit.

APOLLO 15

C David Scott   **LMP** James Irwin
CMP Alfred Worden

△ Endeavor   🕷 Falcon

🚀 Jul. 26, 1971   🧑‍🚀 Jul. 30, 1971   ⏳ Aug. 7, 1971

🚗 17.3 miles (27.9 km)   ◯◯ 169.3 pounds (76.8 kg)

First of the extended "J-series" missions. First use of the Lunar Rover.

APOLLO 16

C John Young   **LMP** Charles Duke, Jr
CMP Thomas "Ken" Mattingly

△ Casper   🕷 Orion

🚀 Apr. 16, 1972   🧑‍🚀 Apr. 21, 1972   ⏳ Apr. 27, 1972

🚗 16.8 miles (27 km)   ◯◯ 211.2 pounds (95.8 kg)

First and only Apollo landing in the lunar highlands. First use of the Moon as an astronomical observatory.

APOLLO 17

C Eugene Cernan   **LMP** Harrison Schmitt
CMP Ronald Evans

△ America   🕷 Challenger

🚀 Dec. 7, 1972   🧑‍🚀 Dec. 11, 1972   ⏳ Dec. 19, 1972

🚗 18.6 miles (30 km)   ◯◯ 242.5 pounds (110 kg)

Last manned mission to the Moon. Geologist Harrison Schmitt is the first professional scientist to fly on an Apollo mission.

July 1969 Apollo 11—first human on the Moon.

November 1969 Apollo 12 crew visit unmanned lunar probe Surveyor 3.

April 1970 Apollo 13—disaster averted.

December 1972 Apollo 17—last manned mission to the Moon.

SPECIFICATIONS

SATURN V

HEIGHT: 363 feet (110.6 m)
DIAMETER: 33 feet (10.06 m)
TOTAL MASS: 6,699,000 pounds (3,038,500 kg)
PAYLOAD (EARTH ORBIT): 260,000 pounds (118,000 kg)
PAYLOAD (LUNAR ORBIT): 103,600 pounds (47,000 kg)

Instrument unit This ring of electronic gear started and stopped the engines, guided the rocket in flight, and communicated data back to Earth.

Lunar Module The Lunar Module was tucked away above the top S-IVB stage for launch. It was pulled free by the Command Module once in space.

Command Module Three astronauts lived and worked here during their journey to and from the Moon.

S-IVB third stage This single engine stage was used to propel the Apollo spacecraft away from Earth orbit and toward the Moon.

S-II second stage The second stage fired for six minutes, boosting the third stage and the Apollo spacecraft to an altitude of 114 miles (183 km).

Launch escape tower This solid-fuel rocket could lift the Command Module away from the Saturn V in an emergency (it was never used).

Service Module This supplied the Command Module with oxygen, electricity, and rocket power. It was jettisoned just before re-entry into Earth's atmosphere.

Fuel tank Flammable fuel or liquid oxygen was held in an insulated tank to keep these super-cold liquids from turning to gas.

Saturn V Rocket

To get to the Moon you had to think big. Accelerating three astronauts and their spacecraft to a speed fast enough to leave Earth's gravity took a lot of power. In the nine minutes it took the Saturn V rocket to climb into space it burned up enough liquid fuel and liquid oxygen to fill one and half Olympic-size swimming pools. The force of the rocket was powerful enough to lift 500 elephants off the ground. Yet, despite the towering size of the Saturn V, at the end of the Moon mission only the small Command Module, with its three astronauts aboard, returned intact to Earth. Everything else either fell back to Earth, hit the Moon, or was left on the Moon.

THE BIGGEST ROCKET

Though the last Saturn V flew in 1973, this monster rocket still holds the record as the biggest rocket ever built, towering 60 feet (18 m) higher than the Statue of Liberty in New York. It dwarfed all earlier rockets—more than triple the height of the Gemini Titan and over four times taller than the Mercury Atlas rockets.

WERNHER VON BRAUN

Though a rocket as complex as the Saturn V is the work of hundreds of people, the person most responsible for its design and construction was Wernher von Braun. During World War II he had built the German V2 rocket, then, after the war, moved to the United States. In the 1950s von Braun even worked with Walt Disney on TV shows about our future in space.

Rocket engine The first and second stages each had had five huge F-1 rocket engines. These burned fuel and liquid oxygen, creating hot gases rushing out of five giant nozzles.

Fins These helped the rocket fly straight through the air. A titanium skin protected them from 2,000°F (1,100°C) temperatures during ascent.

S-IC LOX tank Cold liquid oxygen (LOX) allowed the liquid kerosene fuel to burn even in the near-vacuum of space.

Saturn V

Missions to the Moon required a new rocket be built just for the job, as no existing rocket was big enough. NASA built 15 Saturn Vs, though two never flew; they became museum exhibits.

S-IC fuel tank Kerosene was the main fuel. When it was burned with liquid oxygen, superhot exhaust gases propelled the rocket upward.

SATURN V

Interstage The three rocket stages were connected by structures called interstages. When the stages separated they broke away and fell back to Earth.

Gemini capsule Took a pair of astronauts into orbit.

S-IC first stage The first stage fired for two and a half minutes, boosting the upper stages and the Apollo spacecraft to an altitude of 38 miles (61 km).

Gemini

Before Apollo came the series of Gemini missions in the mid-1960s that launched two astronauts into orbit around Earth. These used another converted missile, the Titan II, still tiny compared to the Saturn V.

Titan II rocket Launched 10 manned Gemini missions.

TITAN II

Mercury capsule Took a single astronaut into Earth orbit.

Mercury

The one-person Mercury missions that first took American astronauts into orbit in the early 1960s used a converted missile called the Atlas, first designed to launch nuclear bombs around the world.

Atlas D rocket Launched five manned Mercury missions.

ATLAS D

SPECIFICATIONS

MERCURY ATLAS D

HEIGHT: 82 feet (25 m)
DIAMETER: 10 feet (3.05 m)
TOTAL MASS: 259,550 pounds (117,730 kg)
PAYLOAD (LOW EARTH ORBIT): 2,990 pounds (1,360 kg)

SPECIFICATIONS

GEMINI TITAN II

HEIGHT: 103 feet (31.4 m)
DIAMETER: 10 feet (3.05 m)
TOTAL MASS: 339,500 pounds (154,000 kg)
PAYLOAD (LOW EARTH ORBIT): 3,600 pounds (1,630 kg)

T-28:00:00 Official countdown begins
T-27:30:00 Installation of rocket flight batteries begins
T-16:00:00 Rocket safety checks begin
T-11:30:00 Emergency rocket self-destruct devices installed

T-09:00:00 Scheduled six-hour countdown hold begins
T-08:15:00 Start loading rocket fuel
T-05:02:00 Flight crew medical examination
T-04:32:00 Flight crew has breakfast

Countdown

The rocket, the spacecraft, the astronauts, and the work of thousands of people all come together here, at Cape Canaveral, Florida. This is launch day, when three astronauts will experience the ride of their lives as they roar away from Earth to head to the Moon. During the countdown, mission controllers check over every system. Is the rocket working? Is the weather fine? Are all tracking stations ready? Are all computers communicating? Is everything powered up? What if they have to abort the launch? Are all emergency systems ready? One "No-Go" call from a launch controller and there will be no launch today. But everything is Go!

Ready to move
The stack is assembled next to a launch tower. It has several arms that allow technicians to reach the rocket and astronauts to climb aboard the spacecraft.

Building the rocket
Several months before each mission, the three sections of the Saturn V rocket arrive at Cape Canaveral by boat and by aircraft. They are brought to the Vehicle Assembly Building, where several Saturn V's could be assembled at once. Giant cranes lift the rocket parts into position to be joined into one tall "stack." The Apollo spacecraft is placed on top of the Saturn V.

Rolling out
Two months before launch the Saturn V and the launch tower roll out toward the pad. The move is made by a giant tractor called the transporter that crawls along at no more than 1 mile per hour (0.6 km/h).

WATCHING THE CLOCK

The final countdown for an Apollo launch begins at T minus 28 hours. (The "T" is from the early days of rocketry; it stands for test.) The clock is stopped at scheduled times for "built-in holds" to fix technical problems. So the actual time from start of countdown to launch is always longer than 28 hours.

T-03:57:00 Flight crew dons space suits
T-03:00:00 30-minute countdown hold begins
T-02:55:00 Flight crew arrives at launch pad
T-02:40:00 Flight crew boards the Command Module
T-01:55:00 Mission Control center links to spacecraft checked
T-00:42:00 Launch escape system armed
T-00:40:00 Final launch vehicle range safety checks begin
T-00:15:00 Spacecraft switched to internal power
T-00:06:00 Space vehicle final status checks
T-00:05:00 Spacecraft access arm fully retracted
T-00:03:10 Automatic launch sequencer system activated

T-00:00:50 Rocket switched to internal power
T-00:00:10
T-00:00:09 Engine ignition sequence begins
T-00:00:08
T-00:00:07

On the pad

Once at the launch pad, the rocket's tanks are filled with explosive fuel and liquid oxygen and all its systems are checked and rechecked. A team of 500 people at computer stations in the nearby Launch Control Center watch over the preparations.

T-00:00:06
T-00:00:05
T-00:00:04
T-00:00:03
T-00:00:02

Launch morning

T minus 5 hours—a doctor checks out the crew. T minus 4.5 hours—the crew has breakfast, usually steak and eggs.
T minus 4 hours—the astronauts are helped into the space suits they will wear during launch. T minus 3 hours—they are driven to the pad, where a fast elevator takes them to the top of the launch tower. T minus 2 hours, 40 minutes—the crew climbs into the Command Module. They wait for liftoff.

All engines running

T-00:00:04
T-00:00:03
T-00:00:02 All engines running
T-00:00:00 Liftoff!

Liftoff!

Thousands of spectators at the Cape and, through television, millions of people around the world watch as the countdown reaches T minus 10, 9 … The Saturn V engines ignite with the power of a small nuclear bomb. T minus 8, 7, 6 … Gases rushing out the five giant nozzles build up thrust for nine seconds. T minus 5, 4, 3 … With the engines at full power, latches release and the rocket is standing free. T minus 2, 1, 0 … We have liftoff! The Saturn V begins to lift from the pad and rises on a column of flame. T plus 12 seconds … The rocket clears the tower and begins its climb into space. The acceleration makes the astronauts feel four times heavier. They are on their way to the Moon.

TEAM EFFORT

Hundreds of technicians at the Kennedy Space Center at Cape Canaveral supervise the launch of a Moon-bound rocket. Their job is finished once the Saturn V rocket clears the launch tower, allowing the launch controllers time to relax and congratulate themselves on a job well done. From the moment the rocket clears the launch tower, control of the mission is handed over to the Johnson Space Center in Houston, Texas.

In the control room

The control center contains three identical firing rooms, each with 450 computer stations. Technicians can prepare up to two other rockets even while the countdown and launch are underway for the current mission.

Liftoff

Dozens of remote cameras record each launch, many at places, such as here at the top of the launch tower, where no human can stand—the hot gases and sound will kill anyone too close to the rocket.

The launch spectacular

Each Apollo launch attracts hundreds of thousands of people who camp out for days beforehand hoping for a good view. Most people watch from roads and highways 7 to 12 miles (11–19 km) from the launch pad. But astronauts' families, the news media, and politicians watch from a VIP area just 3 miles (5 km) from the pad. In the photo below former President Lyndon B. Johnson (in the dark suit) and other VIPs watch the Apollo 11 launch. It is July 16, 1969.

Hot ticket

Getting into the VIP viewing area required a special pass issued by NASA. These become cherished souvenirs of this historic event.

№ 6306

The National Aeronautics and Space Administration cordially welcomes you to the launch of Apollo 11, the first mission planned to land Man on the Moon and return him safely to Earth.

Kurt H. Debus, Director
Kennedy Space Center, NASA

This credential is issued to the bearer for his sole, exclusive, personal use, and is not transferable. After launch, it may be kept as a souvenir of the mission.

Mission Control

Although the three Apollo astronauts received all the attention during a Moon mission, their flight could not have happened without the effort of hundreds of workers on the ground, many at NASA's Mission Control in Houston, Texas. Before each mission, flight controllers practiced for every failure imaginable, so if something went wrong during a flight they would be ready. Mission Control could abort a mission or a planned activity if they decided it was too dangerous to proceed. All the astronauts were well trained, but they still relied on Mission Control for advice and help, and for permission to "Go" at each critical stage.

Precise timing
They had some of the most powerful computers in the world, but mission controllers used a simple stopwatch to time critical events, such as engine burns and lunar landings, to ensure the astronauts did not run out of fuel.

Control console
Computer screens provided constant feedback on how well the spacecraft systems were working. Warning lights flashed if something was abnormal.

Projection systems Projection equipment for the display screens was kept here. The controllers called this room the "bat cave."

Screens Large display screens showed mission status and live TV images.

NERVE CENTER

Here, in Mission Control's main room, dozens of people watched over each mission, backed up by hundreds of other experts in the "back rooms." Each console controller monitored one part of the spacecraft and reported to the Flight Director if everything was "Go!" or if something was wrong.

1 Director of Flight Operations: oversaw Mission Control.
2 Mission Director: represented NASA Headquarters.
3 Department of Defense Representative: was responsible for military matters such as the recovery ships.
4 Public Affairs Officer: was the television and radio voice of Mission Control.
5 Flight Director: led the team from just after liftoff to splashdown, and was responsible for crew safety.
6 Instrumentation and Communications Officer: monitored the Apollo spacecraft's communications systems.
7 Operations and Procedures Officer: was responsible for Mission Control systems.

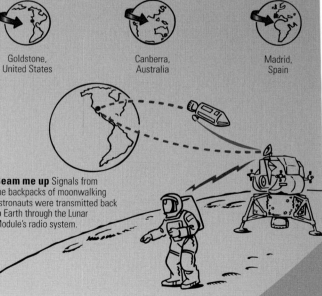

Watching over Apollo
During a mission the main control room in Houston was a busy place. It was staffed round the clock by controllers who carefully monitored performance. Data from sensors on the spacecraft and on the astronauts themselves was constantly beamed back to Earth.

Control consoles Each console monitored part of the spacecraft systems.

Viewing gallery Astronauts' families and special guests could watch the mission from here.

18

13 10

9

5 2 3

1

4

KEEPING IN CONTACT

A network of large dish antennas at tracking stations around Earth received radio signals from the Apollo craft. Contact with Apollo was continuous, but signals took about 1.5 seconds to travel between Earth and the distant Moon, causing an awkward three-second delay in two-way conversations.

Goldstone, United States

Canberra, Australia

Madrid, Spain

Beam me up Signals from the backpacks of moonwalking astronauts were transmitted back to Earth through the Lunar Module's radio system.

8 Assistant Flight Director: took over from Flight Director in his absence.

9 Flight Activities Officer: watched that the crew performed all tasks on time.

10 Network Controller: watched over worldwide network of tracking stations.

11 Flight Surgeons: monitored crew health.

12 Spacecraft Communicator: an astronaut and the only person allowed to talk directly to the astronauts in space; known as "Capcom."

13 Vehicle Systems Engineers: monitored all systems on the spacecraft.

14 Booster Systems Engineer: monitored the Saturn V rocket during the launch.

15 Retrofire Officer: planned aborts and options to return to Earth.

16 Flight Dynamics Officer: planned spacecraft moves and recommended whether to "Go" or "Abort" a mission.

17 Guidance Officer: monitored spacecraft guidance and navigation systems.

18 Maintenance and Operations Supervisor: looked after equipment at Mission Control.

19 Experiments/Lunar Surface Operations Officer: directed science activities during moonwalks.

Journey to the Moon

The journey to the Moon and the return each took three days. The three astronauts were strapped into their seats and wore full space suits only for the launch and landing. During the trip they spent most of their time working, eating, and sleeping in the Command Module. Space was tight but the men were weightless and could float around the cramped interior, finding room to stretch out. On the way to the Moon the astronauts fired small guidance rockets to check their course, prepared the Lunar Module for landing, and sent back television broadcasts showing Earth getting smaller and the Moon getting larger. The astronauts' schedule was busy—they slept for only about five hours a day.

Space hatch
Astronauts boarded the Command Module then, after splashdown, left it through the side-mounted air-tight hatch. It had one of the five Command Module windows.

COMMAND AND SERVICE MODULE

The main Apollo spacecraft consisted of the cone-shaped Command Module attached to the cylindrical Service Module. The astronauts lived in the Command Module. The Service Module contained a rocket that fired once to slow the craft and place it into orbit around the Moon and again to boost it out of lunar orbit and back to Earth.

Engine nozzle The main rocket was fired when entering and leaving lunar orbit and occasionally for mid-course corrections.

FACT FILE

NASA spacecraft evolved very quickly in the 1960s from the small one-person Mercury capsule to the two-person Gemini craft that orbited Earth, and then to the more spacious Apollo Command and Service Module combination, which accommodated three astronauts on a trip to the Moon or to the Skylab space station that flew in the early 1970s.

Mercury
Six Missions
1961–63

Gemini
Ten missions
1965–66

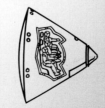

Apollo
Fifteen missions
1968–75

4,000 ENGINEERS
to design and build the Apollo spacecraft.

Flying Apollo

The Apollo control system seems old-fashioned by today's standards—the spacecraft's computers had less computing power than the cell phones of today, and its displays were mostly simple gauges. Yet, with the Command Module's crude computers, 24 instruments, 566 switches, and a small telescope for sighting stars, astronauts were able to fly the spacecraft accurately to the Moon and back.

JIM LOVELL

> Flying to the Moon there was no day and night, and the Sun was always up; the sky was always black, the Earth was just a spot, and so was the Moon.

APOLLO 8 AND 13

Propellant tanks These large tanks stored fuel for the Service Module's main engine.

Reaction control rockets These rockets were used for turning and aiming the combined Command and Service Module.

Direction rockets These small rockets were used for turning and aiming the Command Module.

Access tunnel This linked the Command Module and the Lunar Module.

Oxygen and hydrogen tanks Gases in these tanks supplied air for the crew and generated electricity.

Deep space antenna This four-dish antenna was used for communicating with Earth.

Service Module This contained the fuel, oxygen, and life-support systems.

Command Module This is where the crew lived during the journey.

Parachute Three parachutes slowed the Command Module as it landed back on Earth.

5 YEARS
from the first plans to the first complete spacecraft.

3 ASTRONAUTS
to fly Apollo to the Moon and back.

102:45:25 <u>ALDRIN</u>: 4 forward. 4 forward. Drifting to the right a little. 20 feet, down a half.

102:45:31   <u>MISSION CONTROL</u>: 30 seconds.
(30 seconds of fuel left until the landing has to be aborted.)

102:45:32   <u>ALDRIN</u>: Drifting forward just a little bit; that's good.

Touchdown

The first Moon landing, on Sunday, July 20, 1969, was dramatic. As Apollo 11's Neil Armstrong and Buzz Aldrin piloted their Lunar Module, Eagle, to the surface, alarms went off warning that the computer was overloaded. Abort the mission? Mission Control quickly replied, "You are 'Go' for landing!" Armstrong realized the autopilot was taking them into a field of large boulders. He took control, flew over the boulders and landed with just 20 seconds of fuel remaining. Mission controllers were on the edge of their seats. "You got a bunch of guys about to turn blue," said Capcom Charlie Duke, "We're breathing again." They had done it. Five more missions repeated their success.

Planting the flag
Early in their moonwalk, Neil Armstrong and Buzz Aldrin planted the American flag in lunar soil. While no nation can claim the Moon as its own, this act, repeated by every other Apollo crew, recognized that this was a proud American achievement.

102:45:40 <u>ALDRIN</u>: Contact Light.
(The lander has touched the lunar surface.)

102:45:43 <u>ARMSTRONG</u>: Shutdown

102:45:44 <u>ALDRIN</u>: Okay. Engine Stop.

102:45:45 <u>ALDRIN</u>: ACA out of Detent.

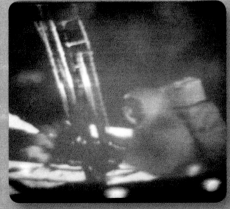

Live from the Moon
Neil Armstrong's first steps on the Moon were recorded by a small black-and-white television camera on the outside of the Lunar Module. The image quality was poor but it thrilled hundreds of millions of people around the globe.

102:45:46 ARMSTRONG: Out of Detent. Auto.

102:45:47 ALDRIN: Mode Control, both Auto.
Descent Engine Command Override,
Off. Engine Arm, Off. 413 is in.

They did it!
Every newspaper in the world
celebrated Apollo 11's success
in large type. Even today, most
people old enough can recall
where they were when humans
first landed on the Moon.

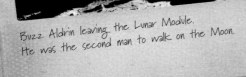
Buzz Aldrin leaving the Lunar Module.
He was the second man to walk on the Moon.

102:45:57 MISSION CONTROL: We copy
you down, Eagle.

102:45:58 ARMSTRONG: Engine arm
is off. (Pause) Houston,
Tranquility Base here.

The Eagle has landed.

Lunar Module

Landing on the Moon required a special spacecraft just for that purpose, the Lunar Module. It did not look like a streamlined spaceship from the movies. The Moon has no air so the lander did not need to be aerodynamic. Instead, engineers designed the Lunar Module in an odd shape dictated by the rocket engines, fuel tanks, and pressurized compartment for two astronauts. The Lunar Module had two parts: the lower "descent stage" contained the legs, fuel tanks, and rocket engine for landing on the Moon. It also stored the tools, experiment packages, and Rover used on the surface. The "ascent stage" had its own rocket engine and used the descent stage as a launch pad, blasting off to return the astronauts to the Command and Service Module.

Radar antenna This antenna was used for judging distance to the Command Module.

High gain antenna This antenna was used for communicating back to Earth.

Window A window each gave the astronauts a view of the landscape when landing.

Forward hatch Astronauts exited the Lunar Module through this opening.

Ladder The ladder was so light that it would have collapsed under the weight of an astronaut on Earth.

Descent stage engine This engine was used for landing on the Moon.

SPACE FOOD

Astronauts ate pre-cooked food from meal-size packages organized by each meal. Some meals were ready to eat; others needed water added. The Command Module's hot water provided hot meals, but all meals in the Lunar Module were cold. Most meals were eaten with a spoon.

Breakfast
Fruit-flavored cereal

Lunch
Pineapple fruitcake

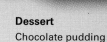

Dinner
Beef and vegetables

Dessert
Chocolate pudding

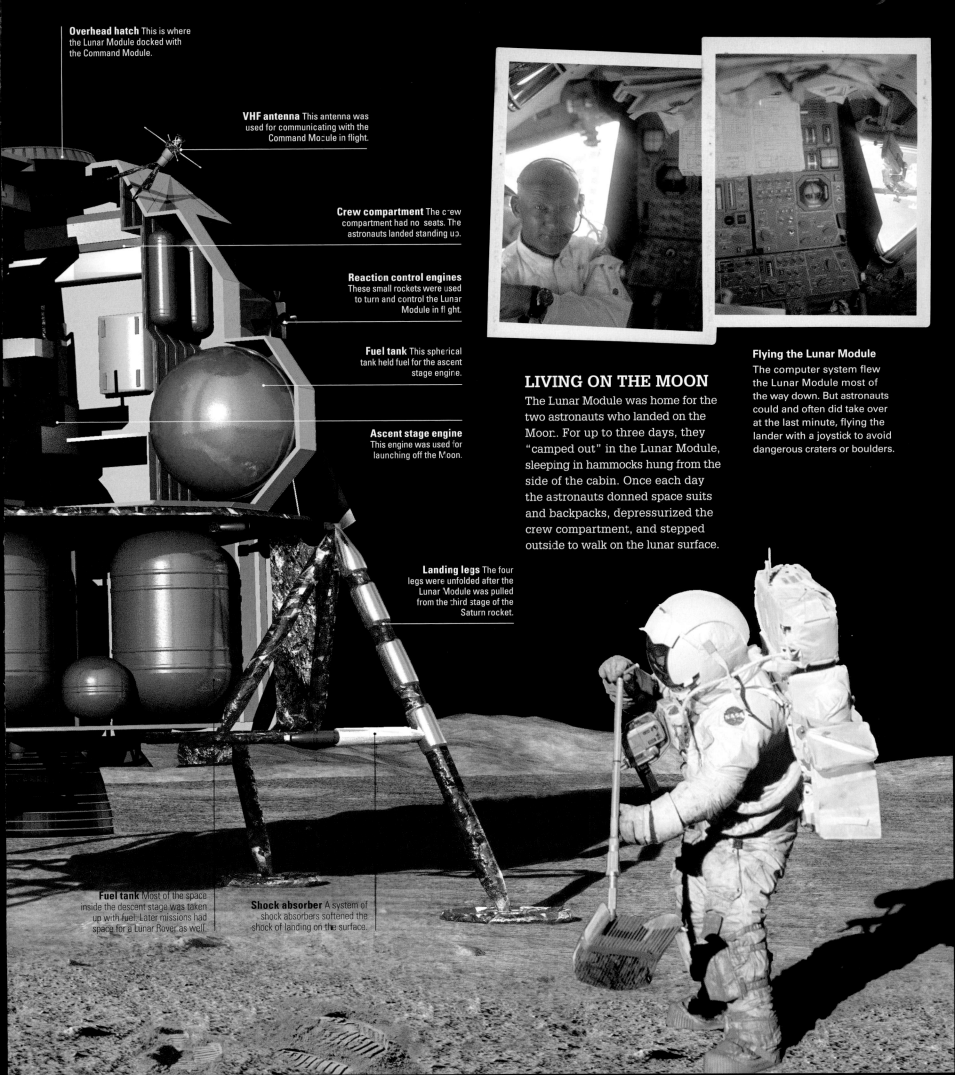

Overhead hatch This is where the Lunar Module docked with the Command Module.

VHF antenna This antenna was used for communicating with the Command Module in flight.

Crew compartment The crew compartment had no seats. The astronauts landed standing up.

Reaction control engines These small rockets were used to turn and control the Lunar Module in flight.

Fuel tank This spherical tank held fuel for the ascent stage engine.

Ascent stage engine This engine was used for launching off the Moon.

Landing legs The four legs were unfolded after the Lunar Module was pulled from the third stage of the Saturn rocket.

Fuel tank Most of the space inside the descent stage was taken up with fuel. Later missions had space for a Lunar Rover as well.

Shock absorber A system of shock absorbers softened the shock of landing on the surface.

LIVING ON THE MOON

The Lunar Module was home for the two astronauts who landed on the Moon. For up to three days, they "camped out" in the Lunar Module, sleeping in hammocks hung from the side of the cabin. Once each day the astronauts donned space suits and backpacks, depressurized the crew compartment, and stepped outside to walk on the lunar surface.

Flying the Lunar Module
The computer system flew the Lunar Module most of the way down. But astronauts could and often did take over at the last minute, flying the lander with a joystick to avoid dangerous craters or boulders.

Exploring the Surface:
Apollo 11

On July 20, 1969, at 9:56 p.m. Eastern Daylight Time, humans first set foot on another world. Neil Armstrong stepped off the pad of the Lunar Module and onto the surface of the Moon in his famous "one small step for a man, one giant leap for mankind." At first he was tethered to the ladder because no one knew if the surface would be like quicksand, but he soon found it was easy to walk around. Armstrong's immediate task was to grab a sample of rocks and soil, in case he had to leave in a hurry. All went perfectly. Buzz Aldrin joined Armstrong on the surface about 20 minutes later and helped to set up experiments and gather more rocks.

Famous footprint
Buzz Aldrin photographed his footprint to record the properties of the lunar soil. His boot left a sharp outline in what looked and behaved like fine talcum powder. The image became one of the most famous photos ever taken—a symbol of the human need to explore.

Off the cuff
A cuff checklist reminded Neil Armstrong of every task he had to perform during the short but busy moonwalk.

East crater pan
Neil Armstrong walked 200 feet (60 m) from the Lunar Module to take this photo panorama of the landing site.

Carrying out experiments
Buzz Aldrin carried two experiment packages away from the Lunar Module. He found it easier to move in one-sixth gravity than anyone had thought.

FIRST FORAY

Mankind's first exploration of another world was a cautious exercise. Armstrong and Aldrin did not venture far from the Lunar Module. This illustration maps their exploration against a standard soccer pitch.

Lunar Module

KEY

⊡ Seismometer

📷 TV camera   ● Neil's panorama photo position   ⬭ Rocks   — Old, shallow crater   — Relatively sharp crater   〜 Disturbed ground

2½ HOURS
Time spent outside the Lunar Module on the Moon's surface.

47.8 POUNDS
(21.7 kg) Earth weight of lunar samples collected.

Lunar science projects
The astronauts set up three science experiments on the Moon: a reflector to bounce laser beams back to Earth, a foil "flag" to collect solar particles, and a seismometer to measure moonquakes.

Exploring the Surface:
Later Missions

Every mission after Apollo 11 became more ambitious, landing at more mountainous sites, with astronauts traveling farther from the Lunar Module. Apollo 12 astronauts visited the Surveyor 3 probe. Apollo 14 astronauts wheeled a tool cart to collect debris from a young impact crater. Apollo 15 used the Lunar Rover to drive up the side of towering Mount Hadley. Apollo 16 landed in the rugged highlands near Descartes Crater. Apollo 17 astronauts drove nearly 5 miles (8 km) from the lander in their longest treks. All moonwalks were tightly scheduled. Astronauts had to work quickly, and if they found something unexpected, Mission Control might grant them no more than a few extra minutes before they had to move on.

CHEAT SHEETS

On later missions with long, complex moonwalks, astronauts had little flipbooks on their suit cuffs. The pages of notes and diagrams reminded them what to do at every stop along the way.

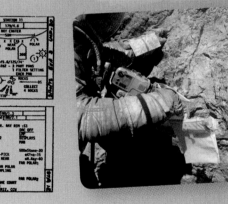

Step-by-step
Here, Apollo 16 astronaut Charlie Duke samples a large boulder. The open flipbook pages list the correct camera settings for a photo panorama.

Day on the Moon
Moon exploration involved lots of walking or driving, sampling, and photography. In the photo below, Jack Schmitt from Apollo 17 is running to the Rover. The field of boulders was created by an ancient meteorite impact.

It's a dirty job

Exploring the Moon was tough and dirty work. At the end of a long day on the lunar surface, astronauts were exhausted and often in pain. And they were dirty, covered with sooty lunar dust. But they were all sad to leave.

LEFT BEHIND

Astronauts discarded equipment to save weight, but they also left many souvenirs behind. Some, such as Apollo 11's gold olive branch of peace, were official NASA items. Others were personal mementos placed on the surface during brief private moments.

The "Fallen Astronaut"

The Apollo 15 crew left this sculpture and plaque in memory of astronauts who had died in the space race.

We were here

A commemorative plaque was fixed to each Lunar Module descent stage.

Thinking of you

Charlie Duke from Apollo 16 left behind a photo of his family.

On the Moon

Visit the Moon and you will find it an alien place. Because it has no insulating atmosphere, the temperature soars to daytime highs of +240°F (+115°C) then plummets to nighttime lows of −240°F (−150°C). Without air the sky is black, even when the Sun is shining and the landscape is bright. You cannot see any stars until you stand in the shadows and wait for your eyes to adjust. But it is easy to see Earth. Because of its bright clouds, oceans, and polar ice, our planet shines about 60 times brighter in the Moon's sky than the Moon appears in Earth's night sky. For the two weeks of every month when the Sun is below the lunar horizon, "Earthlight" illuminates the moonscape.

Low-g jump
Even with their bulky space suits, astronauts could bound around with ease, thanks to the Moon's low gravity. Here, Commander John Young from Apollo 16 makes a jumping salute.

Clear scenery
Is this a low hill that is just a short hike away? Start walking there and you will be surprised. Mount Hadley is actually higher than any peak in the Rocky Mountains, and you will be marching for hours to reach it. The lack of air makes faraway objects appear as sharp as nearby ones, so it is difficult to judge size and distance.

HOW FAR? HOW HIGH?
How far away do you think Mount Hadley is, and how high above the plain is its peak?

Weight loss
The Moon has six times less gravity than Earth does, so whatever your weight on Earth, you will weigh only one-sixth of that on the Moon.

EARTH
80 pounds
(36 kg)

MOON
13 pounds
(6 kg)

FACT FILE

If we held the Olympic Games on the Moon, all records would be broken. Athletes would be just as strong on the Moon as they are on Earth and they could jump and throw things six times higher and farther.

ANSWER
Distance: 8 miles (13 km)
Height: 14,760 feet (4,500 m)
That is ten times as high as the
world's tallest skyscraper.

There's an Earth out tonight

From any location on the near side of the Moon, Earth hangs in the same place in the sky, never rising or setting, but going through phases over a monthly cycle. This photo shows a "Last Quarter Earth."

Earth view versus Moon view

As seen from the Moon, Earth looks four times larger than the Moon does in our sky.

MOON TEMPERATURE

Astronauts experience temperature extremes within just a few steps, from the baking heat of a surface in bright sunlight, to the deep cold of an area always in shadow. Space suits need to insulate astronauts from these extremes.

Hot and cold

1 Sunlit surfaces can become superhot.
2 Surfaces in shade are supercold.
3 Space itself has no temperature. In a vacuum there is nothing to become hot or cold. Only solids and gases in space have temperature.

Men's javelin
Earth record: 323 feet (98.5 m)
Earth record × 6 = 1,938 feet (591 m)

Men's high jump
Earth record: 8.04 feet (2.45 m)
Earth record × 6 = 48.24 feet (14.70 m)

Women's long jump
Earth record: 24.67 feet (7.52 m)
Earth record × 6 = 148.02 feet (45.12 m)

Space Suit

Officially they are called "extravehicular mobility units," or EMUs. We know them as space suits. They are like small spaceships designed to protect an astronaut from the hazards of space: micrometeorites, radiation, extremes of temperature, and complete vacuum, or lack of air to breathe. The Apollo space suits also had to keep astronauts safe on the lunar surface, but still allow them to walk, bend their arms and legs, pick up rocks, and handle tools. The suits were strong enough to resist damage caused by falling onto sharp rocks, but not so heavy that the astronauts would get tired working inside them.

Lean into it
The life support backpack made up about two-thirds of the weight of an Apollo space suit. To keep from falling over, astronauts had to lean forward.

Lunar leapers
This magazine cover from 1929 shows some athletic explorers on the Moon. Their space suits are made of hard metal plates like medieval suits of armor.

Moon glove
Rubber tips helped moonwalkers grasp tools and rocks. This is one of Neil Armstrong's gloves.

HISTORY OF THE SPACE SUIT

During the early space walks on the Gemini and Voskhod missions, astronauts often became too hot and tired inside their stiff and stuffy space suits. Improved space suit designs allowed Apollo, then Shuttle and Space Station astronauts to work outside for up to eight hours at a time.

1920s Underwater pressure suit
Early deep-sea diving suits served as the model for later suits designed for aviation and space.

1934 High-altitude suit
Aviator Wiley Post used this suit on his pioneering high-altitude aircraft flights in the 1930s.

1961 Yuri Gagarin's space suit
The early Soviet suits allowed cosmonauts to eject from their capsules before landing.

1962 Grumman moon suit
This strange design allowed an astronaut to bring his arms inside to work in the upper "can."

1962 Mercury space suit
Made of aluminized nylon, this design was adapted from a U.S. Navy high-altitude aircraft suit.

INSIDE A SPACE SUIT

The Apollo space suits allowed astronauts to work outside on the airless Moon, in the extreme heat of the Sun and cold in the shade. The bulky suits weighed 200 pounds (90 kg) on Earth but only one-sixth of that on the Moon. Astronauts could jump around with ease.

Portable life support system This backpack supplied oxygen, regulated the space suit temperature, and contained the radios and antennas for communication.

Visor A visor coated with a thin layer of gold shielded against sunburn from the intense ultraviolet light.

Heartbeat Sensors recorded the astronaut's heart rate and oxygen consumption. The data was relayed to a doctor at Mission Control.

Safety seal The heart of the space suit was the pressure garment assembly. It formed an airtight seal against the vacuum of space.

WIRED FOR SOUND This cap was equipped with built-in earphones and microphone.

Urine collection and transfer assembly The contents of this bag were emptied into a waste fluid container in the Lunar Module.

Undergarment The layer against the skin was lined with tubes of flowing water to keep the astronaut cool.

First defense The white outermost layer protected the astronaut from solar radiation and micrometeoroids.

KEEPING COOL Water circulated from the undergarment to the backback where it cooled, and back again.

CALL OF NATURE During moonwalks, urine was collected in a bag worn around the hips. Astronaut underpants were designed to contain solid waste, but the astronauts preferred to wait until they were back in the Lunar Module where they used special stick-on plastic bags.

Moonboots The lunar boots were slipped on over the inner boots of the pressure garment assembly. They had ribbed silicon rubber soles.

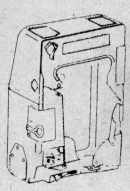
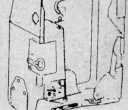

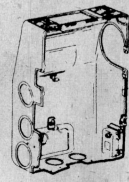

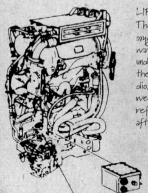

LIFE-SUPPORT BACKPACK The backpack contained tanks of oxygen for the astronaut to breathe, water tanks for the cooling undergarment, and filters for cleaning the oxygen supply of exhaled carbon dioxide. The backpack's batteries were recharged and the tanks refilled inside the Lunar Module after each moonwalk.

Lunar Rover

How do you travel around the Moon? You drive. For the final three Apollo missions, astronauts used a vehicle built like a dune buggy—a "moon buggy"! The Lunar Rover allowed astronauts to travel up to 5 miles (8 km) from the lander, far enough to visit interesting craters but near enough to walk back to the Lunar Module if the Rover broke down (although it never did). Wire-mesh wheels provided good traction on the dusty lunar surface. Each wheel had its own battery-powered electric motor, providing four-wheel drive and four-wheel steering. A television camera and dish antenna sent images back to Earth from each stop along the way.

The Moon bike
NASA tested a Moon motorbike but the Rover was better— it carried more gear and Moon rocks.

LEARNER DRIVERS
Astronauts Dave Scott and Jim Irwin practice Lunar Rover driving in the American desert.

READY TO ROAM

This photo shows Apollo 16 Commander John Young adjusting the Rover's main antenna for a better link with Earth. A map of the area is clipped above the control panel. At the rear of the Rover is a structure for carrying all the geology equipment and lunar samples.

MOON BUGGY DASHBOARD

Like a car, the Rover had a dashboard with instruments to indicate speed and distance covered. Other dials showed the tilt of the Rover. Instead of a steering wheel and pedals, astronauts used a joystick-like T-Handle. They pushed it forward to go, pulled it backward to reverse, or turned it left and right to steer.

Direction and range indicator This showed the direction and the distance traveled.

Sun shadow device The shadow cast by this device was another way to tell direction.

Speedometer This indicated a top speed of 12 miles per hour (20 km/h).

Power and temperature gauges These showed the status of the electric motors.

T-shaped handle The driver accelerated, braked, and steered with this device.

Star of the show

Live television coverage was beamed to Earth via the dish antenna. The camera (wrapped in gold foil) was remotely controlled by an operator at Mission Control.

Quick fix

During Apollo 17, part of the Rover's rear-wheel fender broke off, causing problems with thrown dust. The astronauts made a replacement with some folded maps and clamps.

FACT FILE

On the Apollo 14 mission, astronauts Shepard and Mitchell used a hand-pulled cart called the Modular Equipment Transporter to carry geology tools and Moon rock samples. This helped them travel farther than was possible during the first two missions. However, the real revolution in lunar transport came with the Rovers used in the final three missions.

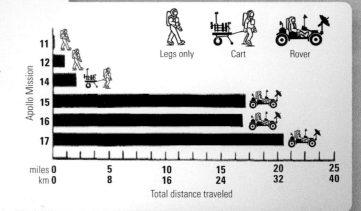

Legs only   Cart   Rover

Apollo Mission

	11
	12
	14
	15
	16
	17

| miles | 0 | 5 | 10 | 15 | 20 | 25 |
| km | 0 | 8 | 16 | 24 | 32 | 40 |

Total distance traveled

Command Module Pilot

While his two friends were exploring the Moon on the surface, the third member of the crew, the Command Module pilot remained in orbit around the Moon. He conducted science observations and looked after his Command/Service Module, making it ready to rendezvous with the Lunar Module when it came back from the Moon's surface. During the time on his own (lasting several days on the last and longest Apollo missions) the Command Module pilot would be out of sight and out of radio contact with Earth on the far side of the Moon for almost half of each two-hour orbit around the Moon. He was completely alone, unable to talk with his fellow astronauts nor anyone on Earth.

TICKET HOME

Only the Command Module was built to return to Earth and survive re-entry. While every Command Module pilot enjoyed his quiet time alone in orbit, each was overjoyed to see the Lunar Module returning and to have his two moonwalking friends safely back on board for the trip back home to Earth.

MOON SHOTS

A prime task of the Command Module pilot was to operate several large film cameras to take thousands of images of the Moon from orbit, to map its surface in detail. These helped scientists determine the ages of the craters, seas, and mountains, and to learn more about how the Moon formed.

Camera shots
The cameras operated by the Command Module pilot returned images of 20 percent of the lunar surface and remain some of the sharpest photos of the Moon ever taken. Shot on film, most are now digitally scanned and available on the Internet.

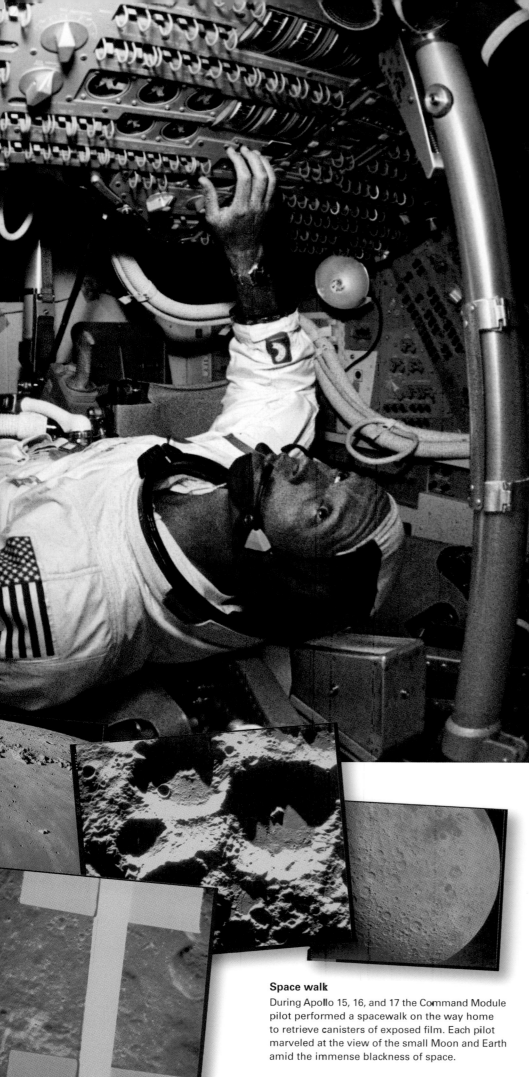

MICHAEL COLLINS

"I knew I was alone in a way that no earthling has ever been before."

COMMAND MODULE PILOT, APOLLO 11

MICHAEL COLLINS

While people remember moonwalkers Neil Armstrong and Buzz Aldrin, Command Module pilot Michael Collins was the indispensable third member of Apollo 11, the first Moon landing.

Space walk

During Apollo 15, 16, and 17 the Command Module pilot performed a spacewalk on the way home to retrieve canisters of exposed film. Each pilot marveled at the view of the small Moon and Earth amid the immense blackness of space.

Splashdown

The last part of the Moon mission is a dangerous one. The Command Module hits Earth's atmosphere at 24,500 miles per hour (39,500 km/h), ten times faster than a rifle bullet. If it hits at the wrong angle it will either burn up or shoot off into space, never to return. If the heat shield fails, the intense heat of re-entry will be fatal. If the parachutes fail to open, the capsule will hit the ocean too hard. If they land too far off course, they could sink before the recovery ship reaches them. But for Apollo 11, and every mission to the Moon, the splashdown worked as planned and the astronauts were soon safe onboard the waiting U.S. Navy aircraft carrier.

SPLASHDOWN AND RECOVERY

Eight minutes after first entering the atmosphere, the Command Module slows down enough for three large parachutes to open. At splashdown, balloons inflate to keep the capsule upright. Navy divers help the astronauts get into baskets to be hoisted into a helicopter that takes them to the waiting ship.

MOON GERMS?

For the first three Moon landings, returning astronauts are whisked into a sealed quarantine trailer where they live for two weeks, isolated from friends and family—even the President. Scientists fear astronauts might catch dangerous germs on the Moon. They never do, so for the later landings the quarantine is cut.

Back on Earth
The Command Module is the only part of the spaceship to return intact to Earth. Its silvery surface is scorched brown by the intense heat of re-entry.

CELEBRATION TIME!

Once they are given a clean bill of health, the astronauts are released to enjoy their celebrity status, commemorated in medallions and souvenirs. Ticker-tape parades, world tours, meetings with presidents and royalty—they are all showered on the famous astronauts. Some describe it as the toughest part of the mission!

U.S. First To Moon
ARMSTRONG - COLLINS - ALDRIN
JULY 20th 1969
APOLLO 11

Apollo 13

On their way to the Moon on April 13, 1970, the Apollo 13 astronauts had just finished a television broadcast to Earth when they heard a loud bang. The meters for oxygen and power levels went to zero. No one knew it at the time, but faulty wiring had caused an oxygen tank in the Service Module to explode. To survive the trip home, the three astronauts had to leave the crippled Command Module, now losing oxygen and power, and live for four days in the Lunar Module, a craft designed to house two astronauts for just two days. Hundreds of NASA staff went into action to work out how to save the crew of Apollo 13.

JACK SWIGERT

Okay, Houston, we've had a problem here.

COMMAND MODULE PILOT, APOLLO 13

The world waits
By 1970, after four successful Moon missions, people were used to astronauts going to the Moon. Apollo 13 again riveted the world's attention on space, and people around the globe anxiously waited for word of the crew's fate.

Improvised fix
Mission Control found a way for the astronauts to construct a filter to clean the Lunar Module's air of deadly carbon dioxide. It was made of spare parts they knew were on board, including a plastic hose, bits of cardboard, and duct tape. It worked!

Waiting in fear
At home Marilyn Lovell, wife of Commander Jim Lovell, listens in despair to the communications from space. In the first day of the crisis, many feared the astronauts would not make it back home.

WHERE IT WENT WRONG

The explosion happened on the way to the Moon (1). The astronauts fired the Lunar Module's engine (designed for landing on the Moon) to put them on a path that looped around the Moon then returned directly to Earth (2). They jettisoned the Lunar and Service modules, powered up the Command Module on its batteries, and re-entered Earth's atmosphere (3).

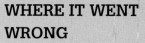

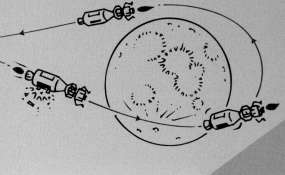

Back on Earth

On April 17, four days after the crisis began, the Apollo 13 Command Module plunged back through Earth's atmosphere, opened its parachutes, and returned the astronauts safely home.

All smiles in Houston

With the astronauts back, mission controllers in Houston celebrated. Their hard work had saved the crew. Astronauts called the Apollo 13 crisis Mission Control's "finest hour."

Moon Rock

More valuable than diamonds or gold are the rough rocks and dusty soil samples collected by Apollo astronauts during their moonwalks and drives. Over six missions, they brought back more than 2,400 samples weighing (on Earth) a total of 842 pounds (382 kg). Many Moon rocks proved to be much older than Earth rocks—the oldest on our planet date back 3.8 billion years, but Moon rocks can be as old as 4.5 billion years, almost as old as the Solar System itself. They are older because, without an atmosphere, water, or moving continents, the Moon's surface has remained unchanged for billions of years. That makes Moon rocks a priceless record of what the Solar System was like in its early years.

WORKING ON THE MOON

Collecting Moon rocks was hard work. The stiff spacesuit made it difficult to bend over and manipulate tools. Here, James B. Irwin on Apollo 15 uses his scoop to make a trench in the lunar soil. Astronauts used many other tools to collect samples.

Precious cargo
Astronauts packed the rocks into air-tight containers that were opened only after they were in a sealed laboratory on Earth. This one, from Apollo 16, contains a rock, some labeled soil sample bags, and a core tube.

Lava rock
All Moon rocks are classed as igneous, or volcanic, having formed from cooling lava early in the Moon's history. This rock is pitted with lots of bubbly holes characteristic of rocks from volcanoes.

STUDYING MOON ROCKS

NASA's Lunar Sample Laboratory in Houston, Texas, contains most of the Moon rocks returned by Apollo, but samples are sent around the world to hundreds of scientists who wish to study the Moon.

Core tube
A tube pounded into the ground captured a core of material from as deep as 10 feet (3 m). On later missions, astronauts used an electric drill to drive in the core tube.

Tongs
Because it was so difficult to bend over in the space suit, astronauts often used finger-like tongs on the end of a long pole to grab rocks.

Scoop
To collect samples of loose soil, astronauts used a scoop. Soil samples were dropped into labeled bags so scientists could tell where each sample came from.

Hammer
Just as geologists do on Earth, astronauts used a hammer to break off parts of rocks too big to pick up or bring back in one piece.

Rake
Astronauts dragged a rake across the surface to gather small rocks. They shook it so the soil fell out, leaving only rocks too big to fall through the rake's teeth.

Gnomon
This device, placed next to a rock, allowed astronauts to document its size, color, and position before they picked the rock up.

Under the microscope
Slicing a thin section from a Moon rock then examining it under a microscope reveals the colorful crystals and minerals that make up the rock. These give scientists clues about how the rock formed.

Astronaut David Scott inspects a Moon rock in the Lunar Sample Lab in Houston.

To avoid contaminating them, Moon rocks are never handled directly.

After Apollo

After the last Apollo mission, the United States ignored the Moon for many years, choosing instead to send unmanned probes to the planets and to develop the early Skylab space station, then the Space Shuttle. However, the Soviet Union continued to send unmanned Luna probes until the mid-1970s. Then the world forgot about the Moon—no spacecraft went there between 1976 and 1990. However, recently there has been a revival of interest in lunar exploration. The United Sates, the European Union, Japan, China, and India have all launched unmanned missions to the Moon in recent years and more are planned.

MAPPING THE MOON

Knowledge gained from the Apollo program and later orbital missions has enabled geologists to create detailed color-coded maps of craters and lunar seas. Each color indicates a different type of mineral or surface composition. These maps are useful for planning where to build future Moon bases.

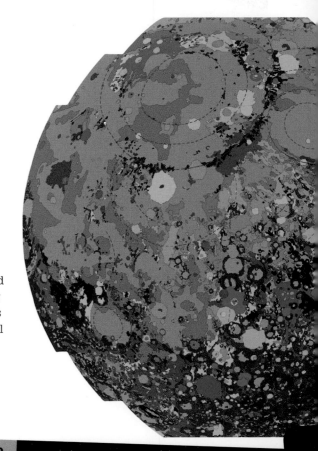

LAST OF THE LUNAS

Between 1970 and 1976 the Soviet Union launched three successful missions to collect lunar soil samples using remote-controlled robot probes. The Soviet Union also launched Lunokhod 1 (November 1970) and Lunokhod 2 (January 1973), the first rovers on another world.

Size comparison
The Lunokhod rovers were about the same size and weight as a compact car. This illustration shows one compared with a 10-year-old boy.

Remote Moon driving

The two Soviet Lunokhod rovers were driven by operators on Earth. They steered the rovers as they watched for obstacles in images sent back every few seconds. Despite the operators' skill, both rovers sometimes got bogged in lunar dust.

The journey of Lunokhod 2

1 Lunokhod 2 arrived at the Moon on top of the Luna 21 spacecraft. Two days after landing, it was driven down a ramp and onto the surface.
2 Guided from Earth, Lunokhod 2 set off on its 23-mile (37-km) journey.
3 The rover was not equipped to directly sample rocks or soil, but it did pause to closely inspect unusual rocks and other features.
4 Lunokhod 2 stopped working after four and a half months. However, its value to science remains. A reflector on the rover bounces laser beams back to observatories on Earth, helping to measure both the exact distance to the Moon and its orbit.

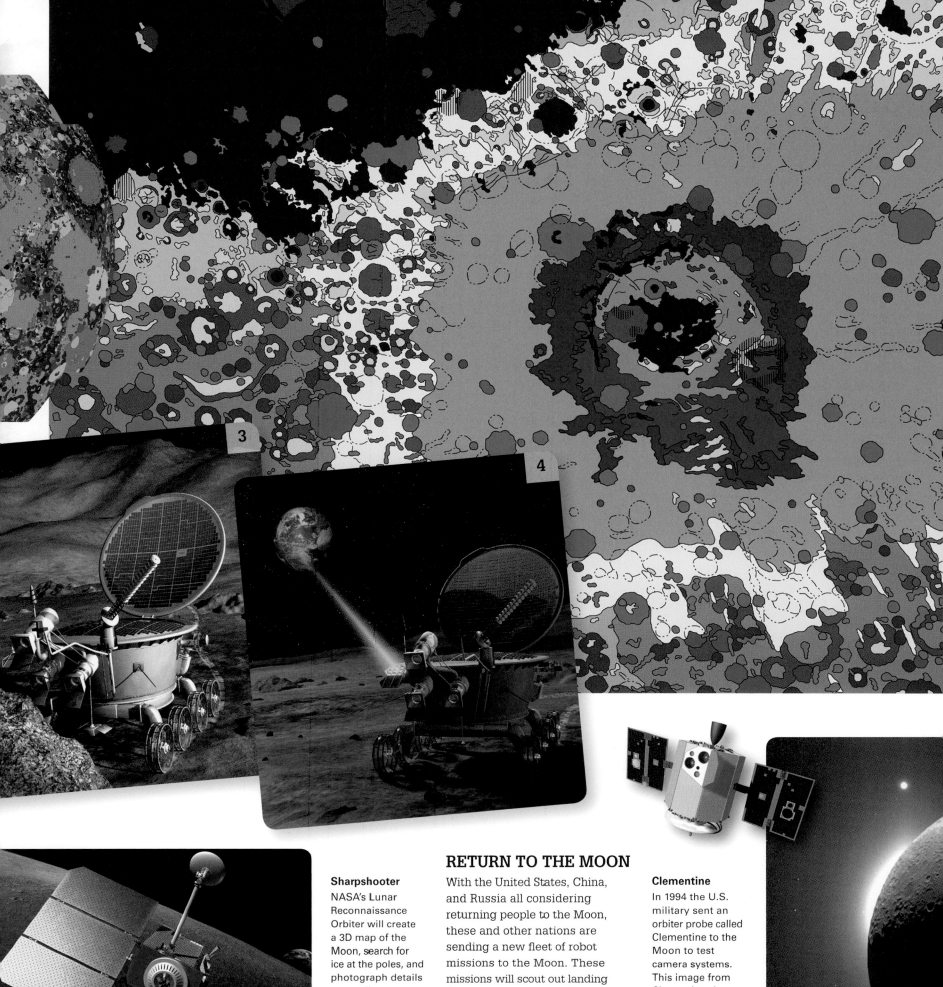

RETURN TO THE MOON

Sharpshooter
NASA's Lunar Reconnaissance Orbiter will create a 3D map of the Moon, search for ice at the poles, and photograph details as small as one meter across—sharp enough to show the landers and rovers left by Apollo.

With the United States, China, and Russia all considering returning people to the Moon, these and other nations are sending a new fleet of robot missions to the Moon. These missions will scout out landing sites and hunt for reservoirs of ice near the lunar poles that could serve as sources of water for astronauts at lunar bases.

Clementine
In 1994 the U.S. military sent an orbiter probe called Clementine to the Moon to test camera systems. This image from Clementine shows the Moon eclipsing the Sun with bright Venus just above the Moon.

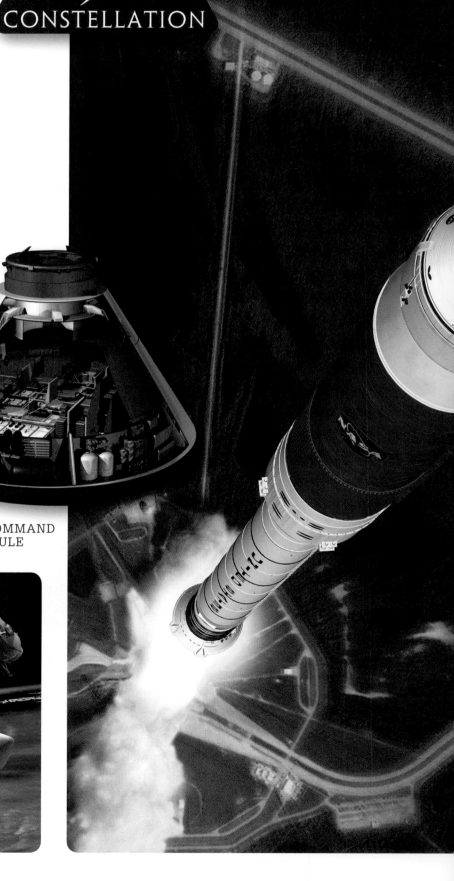

Back to the Moon?

If all goes to plan, astronauts will return to the Moon in 2020. There they will resume the exploration left off by Apollo 17 in December 1972. A program of Moon exploration is part of NASA's Constellation Project, a program to develop replacement spacecraft for the aging Space Shuttle. The Ares V "heavy-lift" rocket will launch the new Altair lunar lander, and the smaller Ares I rocket will launch the Orion crew capsule. Both Ares rockets use parts adapted from the Saturn V and the Space Shuttle. Eventually, these new rockets and spacecraft might be used for a human mission to Mars, most likely as part of an international expedition after 2030.

CONSTELLATION

New look to old designs

The engineers who built the Apollo space hardware got it right. The new Orion Command Module uses the same conical design as the Apollo version but enlarges it. Orion is two and a half times bigger inside, taking six astronauts to the Space Station or four to the Moon.

Ares V cargo launch

A return mission to the Moon begins with the giant Ares V rocket (as powerful as the old Saturn V) launching the unoccupied Altair Lunar Module into orbit around Earth.

ARES V CARGO ROCKET

ARES I CREW ROCKET

ORION COMMAND MODULE

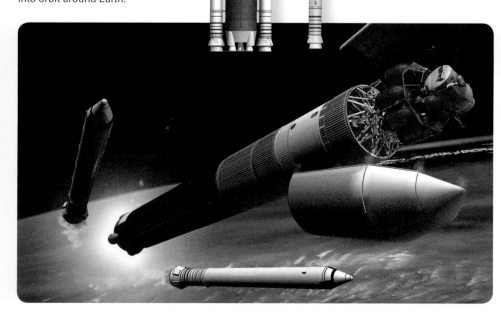

Ares I crew launch

The smaller Ares I rocket, with the Orion Command Module on top, takes the astronauts into Earth orbit. The small abort rockets on top of the capsule can pull Orion free to safety in a launch emergency.

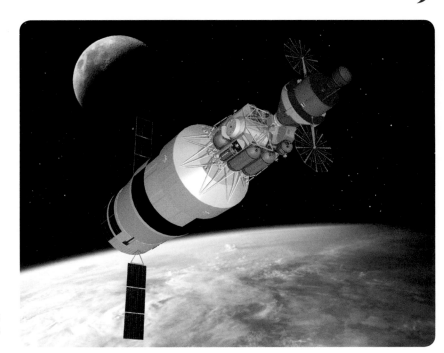

Earth orbit rendezvous

In a plan first considered for Apollo, Orion meets up with the previously launched Altair Lunar Module in Earth orbit. The upper Earth Departure Stage of the Ares V propels both craft to the Moon.

Back on the Moon

All four astronauts from the Orion capsule use Altair to land on the Moon. If the Moon mission proceeds in 2020, humans will return to the lunar surface after an absence of nearly 50 years.

NEW ROCKETS FROM OLD

The Ares rockets use designs from older rockets. The main stage of the Ares I is similar to the Space Shuttle's solid rocket boosters. The main stage of the Ares V uses liquid fuel tanks similar to the Saturn V first stage.

Testing underway
In a ground test, jets of exhaust shoot from the rockets that will be used in the Orion abort system.

Classic hardware
The Ares upper stages use a new version of the J-2 engine from the Saturn V's second stage.

Moon Base

The first astronauts to return to the Moon will stay for up to a week, returning to their Altair lander at the end of each day's excursion. To stay longer and explore farther afield, astronauts will need a permanent base. An all-purpose lander will carry sections of the base to the Moon one at a time, and astronauts will gradually assemble more comfortable living quarters and well-equipped laboratories. Once it is large enough, the base will be staffed all the time with astronauts from many nations arriving for shifts of up to 180 days, as they do now on the International Space Station.

Lunar city
People have been dreaming about living on the Moon for centuries. This artist imagined a whole city built in a crater.

Blow-up base
The first structures on the Moon may be inflatable modules used for living quarters and laboratories. Airtight and offering protection from micrometeorites, the modules would be light, easy to transport to the Moon, and easy for astronauts in space suits to set up. The idea has already been tested in the cold of Antarctica.

Future Moon rover
Astronauts will use large pressurized rovers to reach craters, mountains, and canyons far from their base.

HOME BASE

The first permanent base may be set up at the lunar south pole, on the rim of a crater named after the polar explorer Ernest Shackleton. Near the lunar poles, crater rims receive constant sunlight all month, which can be used to generate power. The crater floors are permanently dark and cold and may contain deposits of water ice, which could provide hydrogen for fuel and oxygen for breathing.

Looking down on the pole
This mosaic of images maps the region around the Moon's south pole, with the actual pole located, just on the edge of Shackleton Crater. The lunar base might be established a few miles away, on a smooth sunlit plateau on the rim of the crater.

Solar power unit →

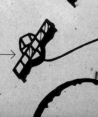

POLE IS THE PLACE
The lunar poles are at the north and south ends of the Moon's axis of rotation. This gives them special advantages as sites for settlement.

Two weeks' sunshine

POLES—high ground always sunny; crater floors always dark and cold.

Two weeks' dark

SOUTH POLE

SHACKLETON CRATER
12 miles (20 km) diameter

LOCATION CHECKLIST

SUN
Lots of uninterrupted sunshine! for generating electricity.

COMMUNICATION
Earth always in sight for communicating with home.

WATER
Ice deposits for drinking water, fuel, and oxygen.

AMUNDSEN CRATER
62 miles (100 km) diameter

EARTH THIS DIIRECTION

BASE LOCATION

BASE OVERVIEW
The first lunar base will likely consist of several connected habitat and laboratory modules. Power will come from solar panels that turn to track the Sun as it circles the horizon through the month. For times when the Sun is not visible, power will come from battery-like storage units called fuel cells.

Habitation

Fuel cells

Crew/cargo lander

Pressurized rover

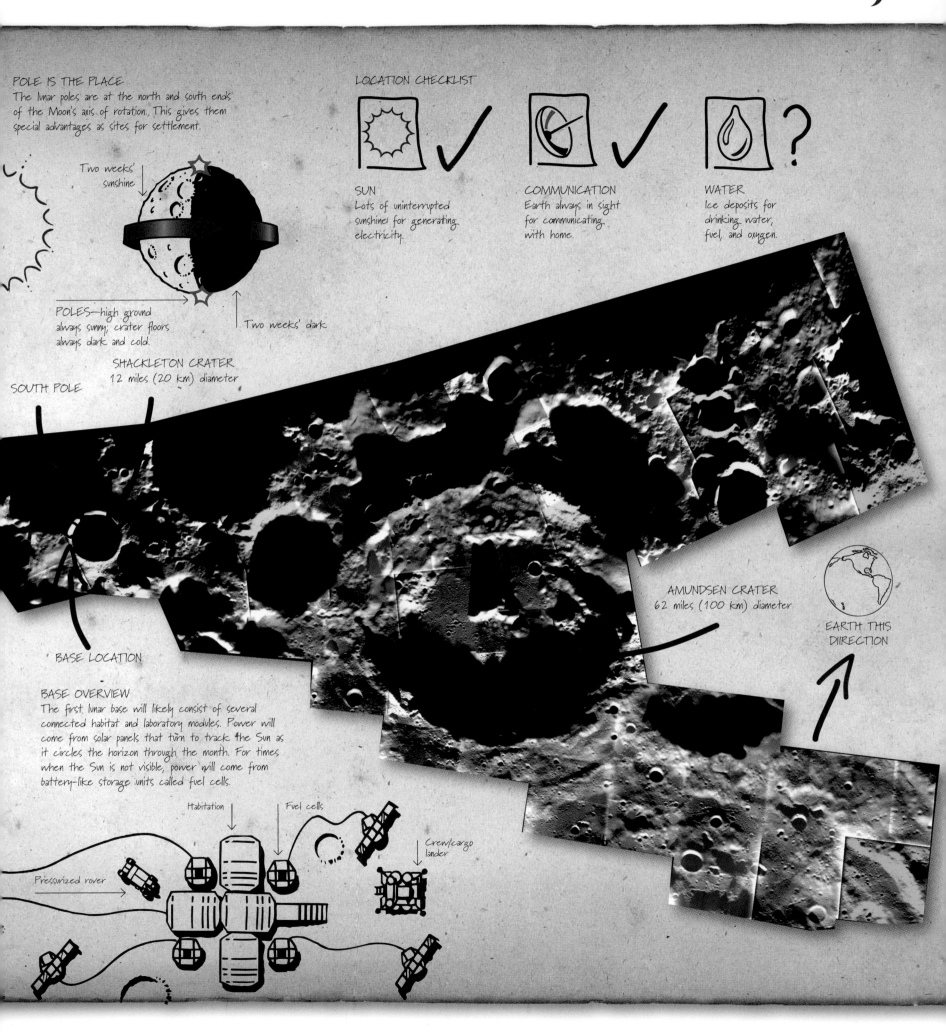

All about the Moon

The Earth–Moon System

We are lucky to have the Moon. Were it not for a rare, catastrophic collision early in Earth's history, we might not have a moon at all—our neighbors Mercury and Venus are moonless. Or perhaps we would have only a tiny moon, like the two little worlds that orbit Mars. Fortunately for us, our moon is large. The Moon's strong gravity stabilizes our planet's spinning axis. Without the Moon, Earth would wobble wildly over millions of years, creating extreme shifts in climate and possibly making it difficult for life to evolve. The lunar gravity also creates ocean tides, which might have helped primitive life to move from the sea onto land.

Moon and Earth compared
The Moon is a little over one-quarter the size of Earth.

Double planet
Our Moon is so big compared to its parent planet Earth that we can think of them as a "double planet." But the bleak, airless Moon could not be more different from the living, watery Earth.

Impact
A protoplanet smashes into the early Earth, perhaps within the first 100 million years after Earth formed about 4.6 billion years ago.

Making the Moon
Rock samples brought back by Apollo astronauts helped solve the mystery of where our Moon came from. Not long after our Solar System formed, it was filled with hundreds of planet-size objects known as protoplanets. One of

FACT FILE

Both the size of Earth and the Moon, *and* their separation are drawn here to scale. The Moon is far away! Traveling at highway speeds, a car would take five months to get there.

Earth   **Car** 5 months

Jet aircraft 3 weeks

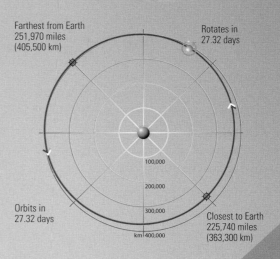

MOON IN MOTION

The Moon takes 27.32 days to orbit Earth. During that time it rotates on its axis once, so the same side of the Moon always faces Earth. The Moon's orbit is not perfectly circular. Its distance from Earth varies by about ten percent.

Farthest from Earth
251,970 miles
(405,500 km)

Rotates in
27.32 days

Orbits in
27.32 days

Closest to Earth
225,740 miles
(363,300 km)

100,000

200,000

300,000

km 400,000

Debris
A ring of debris forms around the primitive molten Earth, giving our planet a short-lived rocky ring system like Saturn's.

A new Moon
The Moon comes together out of the fragments of the giant impact—debris from both the impacting planet as well as from Earth's top layers.

Pull of the tide
The difference in the strength of the Moon's gravity from one side of our planet to the other raises two bulges in the world's oceans. As Earth rotates, each region experiences high and low tides twice a day.

these smashed into the newborn Earth, blasting off part of our planet's rocky outer mantle. The debris re-formed into the Moon.

Apollo spacecraft 3.2 days

Beam of light 1.28 seconds

Moon

Average distance from Earth = 238,860 miles (384,400 km)

Phases of the Moon

Everyone notices the phases of the Moon caused by the Moon's motion around us. At New Moon phase the Moon lies between us and the Sun—the side of the Moon facing us is dark. A few days later the Moon has moved far enough around its orbit and away from the Sun in our sky so that we can see part of its disk lit by the Sun. Each night, as the Moon continues around its orbit, more of its face becomes sunlit. About two weeks after New Moon, the Moon lies opposite the Sun and the lunar face is now fully lit—Full Moon.

Historical explanation
This illustration from 1661 correctly shows how the Moon's phases are a result of its orbit. This was first understood in the 1500s.

Phase shift
As the Moon moves from New to Full phase, it is said to be "waxing." As it moves from Full to New phase, it is said to be "waning."

| New Moon | Waxing Crescent | First Quarter | Waxing Gibbous | Full Moon | Waning Gibbous | Last Quarter | Waning Crescent | New Moon |

A month of phases
This photo series shows the complete cycle of nightly phases, from waxing crescent at top, to Full Moon in the middle, to waning crescent at bottom.

WHEN WORLDS ALIGN

As the Moon orbits Earth it comes between us and the Sun once a month, at New Moon. Usually, the tilt of the lunar orbit causes the Moon to pass above or below the Sun. We get no eclipse. Similarly, at Full Moon, when the Moon lies opposite the Sun, it misses our planet's shadow. But at least four times a year, the Sun, Moon, and Earth align to create some type of eclipse.

SOLAR ECLIPSE

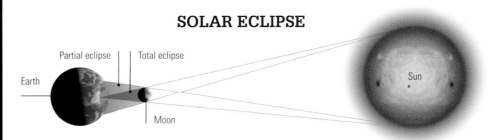

Black Sun
When the Moon passes directly between us and the Sun, it casts its shadow onto Earth. In the outer part of the shadow we see the Moon partly cover the Sun. But in the center of the shadow we see the Moon completely cover the Sun's disk in a total solar eclipse, when only the Sun's faint outer corona remains visible.

LUNAR ECLIPSE

Red Moon
At Full phase the Moon sometimes passes through the shadow our planet casts into space. If it passes completely into the dark, central portion of Earth's shadow, we see a total eclipse of the Moon. The Full Moon gradually darkens then gains an eerie red tint, lit only by dim red light filtering through our planet's atmosphere.

Moon Structure

The Apollo missions taught us a lot about the Moon. Before Apollo no one knew if the Moon was volcanically active, with pockets of magma beneath the crust as on Earth. We now know it is not. Before Apollo no one knew what the inside of the Moon was like. But the astronauts left behind a network of seismometers so scientists could track moonquake waves that traveled through the lunar interior. Some of those moonquakes were set off by Apollo, when the Saturn rockets' third stages and Lunar Module ascent stages were purposely smashed into the Moon like artificial meteorites.

INSIDE THE MOON

Data from Apollo and more recent robot probes suggest that the Moon is a geologically dead world. A cold, hardened crust covers a warm mantle that lacks dense metals. The crust bears the scars of past volcanic activity but no plumes of molten lava erupt today.

THE MOON COMPARED

The Moon is an odd world. None of the other seven planets has a natural satellite as big as our Moon when compared to its parent planet. Only four other moons are larger, but they orbit the gas giant planets Jupiter and Saturn.

Probing the Moon
NASA's GRAIL mission (short for Gravity Recovery and Interior Laboratory) will reveal the Moon's interior using two gravity-measuring orbiting probes. It is due for launch in 2011.

	GANYMEDE	TITAN	CALLISTO	IO	MOON
HOME PLANET	Jupiter	Saturn	Jupiter	Jupiter	Earth
DIAMETER	3,270 miles (5,262 km)	3,200 miles (5,150 km)	2,995 miles (4,820 km)	2,264 miles (3,643 km)	2,159 miles (3,475 km)
MOON FACT	Biggest moon in our Solar System	Only moon with a substantial atmosphere	Heavily cratered ancient ice moon	Has at least 80 active sulfur volcanoes	Only world beyond Earth visited by humans

Crust The rocky lunar crust is about 31 miles (50 km) thick on the near side but 46 miles (75 km) thick on the far side. This explains why the far side lacks smooth lava plains—lava was not able to break through the far side's thicker crust.

Mantle The mantle extends down about 600 miles (1,000 km) and is made of light rocky material that becomes hotter with depth. The heat comes from the decay of radioactive minerals.

Core Data from NASA's Lunar Prospector probe in the late 1990s suggest that the Moon might have a small iron core 250 to 600 miles (400 to 1,000 km) in diameter. The iron might be solid or molten.

MOONQUAKES

Though the Moon lacks Earth's shifting tectonic plates, moonquakes still occur. Some are set off as Earth's gravity tugs at the lunar interior, causing it to rise and fall like a tide. Other quakes come from the impact of meteorites. But some strong, long-lived quakes from just below the surface are of unknown origin.

Sensing the shakes

Astronauts on Apollo 11, 12, 14, 15, and 16 left seismometers on the Moon to measure moonquakes. The unit set up by Apollo 11 did not survive the first lunar night, but the other four worked until they were turned off in 1977.

NEAR SIDE

FAR SIDE

Lunar lows and highs

In these Moon maps, purple and blue areas have the lowest elevation, while orange and red zones are the highest. On the near side, the low basins of the maria are clearly revealed in blue. Most of the far side is highlands, except for the deep South Pole–Aitken Basin (the purple region), caused by a giant impact early in the Moon's history.

EUROPA

HOME PLANET	Jupiter
DIAMETER	1,940 miles (3,122 km)
MOON FACT	Ice crust may cover a global ocean of water

TRITON

HOME PLANET	Neptune
DIAMETER	1,681 miles (2,706 km)
MOON FACT	Surface has geysers of liquid nitrogen

TITANIA

HOME PLANET	Uranus
DIAMETER	981 miles (1,578 km)
MOON FACT	Surface has canyons and high cliffs of ice

RHEA

HOME PLANET	Saturn
DIAMETER	951 miles (1,530 km)
MOON FACT	May have a ring system like Saturn

OBERON

HOME PLANET	Uranus
DIAMETER	946 miles (1,523 km)
MOON FACT	Has a 3.7-mile (6 km-) high mountain

Surface Features

When astronauts explored the Moon they found an ancient surface that looked much as it did about four billion years ago. Unlike our active planet, the static, airless Moon preserves a record of events early in the life of the Solar System when lots of asteroids and comets were flying around, smashing into the newly formed planets and moons. Almost all the features on the Moon were made by impacts or by molten lava brought to the surface as the result of impacts. While many small meteors still hit the Moon, big impacts are rare today and lava no longer erupts onto the surface. The Moon is like a dead fossil from billions of years ago.

NAMES ON THE MOON

Lava plains, or "mare" (from the Latin for "sea"), were named in the 1600s and 1700s when astronomers thought they might be filled with water. The names are fanciful and in Latin, such as Mare Tranquillitatus (Sea of Tranquility) or Sinus Iridum (the Bay of Rainbows). Mountain ranges are named after ranges on Earth. Craters are named for astronomers, astronauts, and philosophers.

Charting craters

This map of the Moon is from 1872. By this time, most features visible through a telescope had already been named.

HIGHLANDS

Most of the Moon's surface is bright highlands that have been battered for billions of years by impacts of meteors and asteroids, creating a landscape filled with craters of every size, from 185 miles (300 km) across to as small as just a few feet across. The highlands are the oldest regions of the Moon.

Making craters

Craters are made when a rocky meteor, asteroid, or an icy comet smashes into the Moon, blasting out a hole 10 to 15 times larger than the impacting object. Billions of years ago, Earth was hit as often as the Moon was but because of erosion most craters on our planet have been destroyed.

When an object hits the surface of the Moon, the object and the surrounding rock are instantly vaporized.

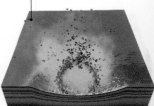

The vaporized rock is thrown into space where it cools and falls back to the Moon in fragments over a wide area.

Spectacular moonscape

The last manned Moon landing, Apollo 17, visited a cratered valley surrounded by the Taurus Mountains. In the distance, astronaut Harrison Schmitt works beside the rover on the rim of Shorty Crater where he discovered bright orange soil. The hills on the horizon are about 3,300 feet (1,000 m) high.

LUNAR SEAS

The dark regions of the Moon are smooth lowland plains, or "mare." These formed when giant impacts cracked the lunar crust, allowing molten lava to erupt onto the surface and flood huge circular basins blasted out by the impacts. The mare are younger than the highlands but are still at least 3.8 billion years old.

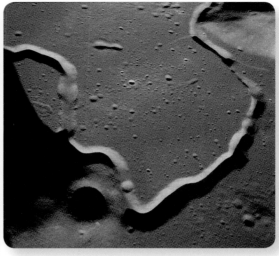

Lunar valleys

Winding valleys, or "rilles," look like they were cut by water but were almost certainly created by molten lava flowing across the surface billions of years ago. This is Hadley Rille seen from orbit during the Apollo 15 mission.

Visiting Hadley Rille

In July 1971 the Apollo 15 astronauts landed next to Hadley Rille and explored along its rim, looking for clues as to how it formed. It was too dangerous to climb down into the deep valley.

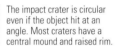
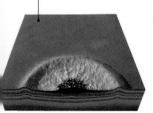

The impact crater is circular even if the object hit at an angle. Most craters have a central mound and raised rim.

Recent impact

Crater Timocharis is a relatively young crater about 20 miles (33 km) across.

THE FAR SIDE

The Moon always has one side turned away from Earth. Spacecraft revealed that this "far side" lacks any large "seas" and is mostly cratered highlands. On the far side the lunar crust may be thicker, preventing lava from erupting onto the surface and forming smooth plains.

Far side farewell

As they left the Moon, Apollo 16 astronauts took this photo showing part of the heavily cratered far side of the Moon.

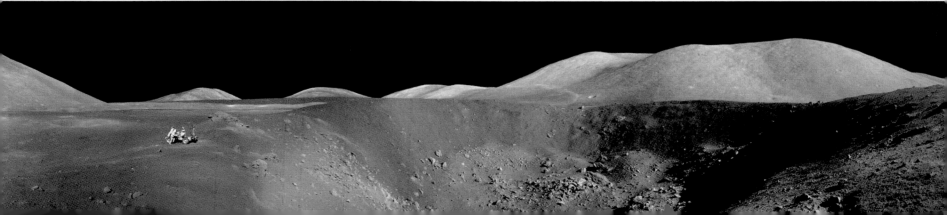

Glossary

abort When a space mission is called off or when a part of a mission is cancelled.

aerodynamic The streamlined shape of a spacecraft, aircraft, or vehicle designed to cut down on drag from the air moving around it.

antenna The device on a spacecraft, often shaped like a dish, that transmits or receives radio and television communications.

asteroid A small rocky object, often irregular in shape, that orbits the Sun. Asteroids are too small to be called planets or dwarf planets.

astronomy The study of the Universe beyond Earth: other planets, stars, and galaxies.

atmosphere The layer of gas that surrounds some rocky planets, such as Earth, or that forms the top layer of gas giant planets, such as Jupiter.

Capcom Short for "capsule communicator," the mission controller, usually an astronaut, whose job it is to talk directly to astronauts in space.

capsule The first crewed spacecraft in the 1960s were bullet-like craft called capsules, unlike the later winged Space Shuttle.

carbon dioxide A gas made of carbon and oxygen. It is exhaled in human breath and can be dangerous if it is concentrated in an enclosed space.

Cold War The era during the 1950s and 1960s when the United States and the Soviet Union considered themselves enemies and often threatened each other.

core The dense central region of a moon or planet, often molten or liquid.

crater The hole blasted onto the surface of a moon or planet by the impact of a meteorite, comet, or other object.

crust The cool, solid layer of a moon or rocky planet, lying on top of a hotter mantle or core.

diameter The distance across the middle of a circle or sphere, measuring how large it is.

docking The term for when two spacecraft meet in space and physically join, often so astronauts can transfer from one spacecraft to the other.

eclipse When one object, or its shadow, hides another—such as when the Moon hides the Sun, or Earth's shadow darkens the Moon.

egress The term for when astronauts exit a spacecraft.

EMU Extravehicular Mobility Unit, the technical term for a space suit.

equator The line around a planet or moon equally distant from the poles. An equator divides a world into northern and southern hemispheres.

EVA Extravehicular Activity, the technical term for when astronauts exit a spacecraft to perform a space walk or moonwalk in their space suits.

far side The side of the Moon always turned away from Earth.

Full Moon The lunar phase when the Moon's disk is fully lit by the Sun.

geologist A scientist who studies rocks, and how the surface features of planets form.

gravity The "force" exerted by all matter that attracts other matter and even energy such as light. Gravity from the Sun keeps all the planets in orbit around the Sun.

heat shield The insulating layer that protects a spacecraft from the intense heat of re-entering the atmosphere.

hemisphere One half of a planetary globe. Globes such as Earth and the Moon are divided into northern and southern hemispheres by an equator.

ingress The term for when astronauts enter a spacecraft.

jettison The act of ejecting or discarding an unneeded spacecraft, to leave it in space or have it crash back to Earth or onto the Moon.

laser An intense light of one wavelength and frequency that can travel long distances.

lava Molten rock that has erupted from the interior of a planet or moon though a volcano or crack in the surface.

lunar The adjective for anything to do with our Moon.

magma Molten rock that remains underground. When it erupts onto the surface, it is called lava.

mantle The middle layer of a moon or planet, between the crust and the core.

mare A Latin word for "sea" used today for the flat lava plains on the Moon.

maria Plural of mare.

mass A measure of how much matter an object contains (Jupiter has more mass than Earth does).

medieval A period of European history from about A.D. 500 to 1500.

meteor The name for the visible streak of light we see when a meteoroid burns up in Earth's atmosphere.

meteorite The name for a small rock that survives its passage through an atmosphere and lands on a planet or moon.

meteoroid The name for small bits of dust and rock orbiting the Sun, which can burn up in an atmosphere.

micrometeoroid A microscopic meteoroid that, despite its small size, can harm a spacecraft or space-suited astronaut because it hits at great speed.

molten The liquid state of superheated rocky or metallic material.

moon Any world that orbits a planet. A moon can be one to thousands of miles across.

NASA The National Aeronautics and Space Administration, the U.S. government agency founded in 1958 that is responsible for space exploration.

New Moon The lunar phase when the Moon passes between Earth and the Sun and is not lit up in our sky.

orbit The circular or elliptical path of a spacecraft around a planet or moon, or a moon around a planet—or of any object traveling around another in space.

payload The cargo, either an unmanned satellite or a crewed spacecraft, that a rocket launches into space.

phase The changes in the appearance of an object, such as the Moon, as we see more or less of it lit by the Sun.

planet Any spherical world orbiting the Sun, or another star, that is large enough to dominate its area of its orbit.

pole The endpoints of a world's axis of rotation, such as the North and South poles on Earth.

pressurized The interior of a spacecraft, sealed from airless space, is filled or "pressurized" with oxygen so astronauts can breathe as they do on Earth.

protoplanet The first large objects to form in the Solar System. Protoplanets crashed together billions of years ago to make the larger planets we know today, including Earth.

quarantine Astronauts returning from the Moon were sealed off, or "quarantined," in an airtight trailer so any extraterrestrial germs they carried could not infect other people.

radiation The term for any form of energy, such as radio, light, infrared, or X-ray.

re-entry The final stage of a spaceflight when a spacecraft flies through Earth's atmosphere at high speed.

revolution The motion of a planet around its star (creating the length of the planet's year) or of a moon around its planet creating the length of the planet's month.

rocket engine A device that mixes rocket fuel and liquid oxygen, ignites it, and forces the gases out a nozzle, propelling the rocket or spacecraft forward.

rocket fuel Combustible liquid fuels, such as liquid kerosene and liquid hydrogen burn when mixed with liquid oxygen and ignited. Some rockets use an explosive solid fuel mixture.

rotation The motion of a planet or moon around its axis, creating the length of its day.

satellite A natural satellite is a moon that orbits a planet. A satellite can also be an artificial probe that orbits a planet or moon.

seismometer A device for measuring earthquakes and tremors, either on Earth or on another world such as the Moon.

simulator Any device designed to provide astronauts with a training experience as close as possible to actual spaceflight.

Solar System The term for the Sun, or any star, and its family of orbiting planets and other objects.

Soviet Union Officially known as the Union of Soviet Socialist Republics, or U.S.S.R., this was a union of eastern European and central Asian Communist states dominated by Russia. It lasted from 1922 until it disbanded in 1991. In the 1960s it was the United States' main rival in space exploration.

space probe A robot craft sent from Earth to explore another planet or moon, or perhaps an asteroid or comet.

spacecraft Any craft, robotic or with a human crew, designed to fly in space.

Sputnik The name of the first satellites launched by the Soviet Union. *Sputnik* is Russian for "traveling companion" or "satellite."

stage (rocket) Large rockets are made of several sections called stages, each with its own engine. The stages fire in sequence one after the other to launch a spacecraft into space.

temperature A measure of how fast molecules and atoms are moving. We feel temperature as how hot or cold something is.

transearth injection The rocket burn that propelled astronauts out of lunar orbit back toward Earth.

translunar injection The rocket burn that propelled astronauts out of Earth orbit toward the Moon.

ultraviolet light Light waves too short for our eyes to see. Ultraviolet light from the Sun causes sunburn.

vacuum The name for any volume with little or no air in it; space is a vacuum.

waning Moon When the Moon is going from Full to New, and its phase is shrinking each night.

waxing Moon When the Moon is going from New to Full, and its phase is growing each night.

zero gravity The term, more correctly called "microgravity," which describes the weightless environment that astronauts experience in space.